"Autographed ... Ch..."

PRINCE OF
Armenia

Nshan A. Erganian
Based on a true story

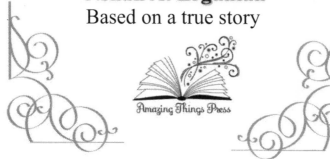

Amazing Things Press

ISBN 978-1949830033

Printed in the United States of America.

For more information, visit

www.amazingthingspress.com

Mary and Nishan circa 1918

With Appreciation

This novel is dedicated to my parents, grandparents, and every Armenian who made the ultimate sacrifice for all Armenians to live in freedom.

For More Information

If you have any questions or would like to contact the author of this book, you can reach him by email at nshan1945@hotmail.com.

Thoughts from the Author

When I first considered writing the story of my father and grandmother's valiant struggle to survive the first recorded genocide of the 20th century, I thought it would be a simpler task than my previous novels. It proved to be just the opposite as I launched into two years of research for information to verify and authenticate the story.

The extensive research was necessary and ultimately added to the book, but it was not nearly as dramatic as the interviews with my father and my uncle, Noray Sarkisian. Their recollections gave a vivid testimony that the Ottoman Empire did, in fact, carry on an initiative to annihilate the Armenian people. It was difficult at times to continue the writing due to the tears blurring my eyes as I listened about men, women, and children having been tortured and murdered only because of their faith and Armenian heritage.

Prince of Armenia is written to honor the legacy of Armenians who sacrificed so much for future generations of our people.

Nshan A. Erganian

"...Go ahead, destroy Armenia. See if you can do it. Send them into the desert without bread or water. Burn their homes and churches. Then see if they will not laugh, sing and pray again. For when two of them meet anywhere in the world, see if they will not create a New Armenia."

William Saroyan

Prologue

It is the first decade of the twentieth century (1900-1910), and there is turmoil throughout the Ottoman Empire. A revolution by a group called the Young Turks has deposed Sultan Abdul Hamid. The Christian nation of Armenia is besieged by Turkish and Kurdish invaders. It is rumored that the new regime has secretly decreed that infant sons of Armenians are to be killed in order to eliminate any future generations. This will become known as the first major genocide of modern times.

My first encounter with death occurs when I am only one year old. The enemy is at my front door. I am Nishan... and this is my story.

Chapter 1
1908

"Hurry, Mary! The soldiers will burst through the door any moment! Dress the boy in a smock and comb out his long hair." My father braces himself against the front door to our home in Amasia, Armenia. A soldier of the Ottoman Empire makes his final demand. My father has stalled the forced entry as long as he possibly can to give my mother time to disguise me as a baby girl. The Ottoman Turks now rule our country and no infant son of an Armenian is safe. I am too young to comprehend the turmoil about to unfold, but I shall hear first-hand stories about it for years to come.

"I can't hold them back any longer, Mary! They're coming in!"

The sound of splintering wood rings in the air as a leather boot kicks the heavy wooden door. It swings open and hangs there on its hinges. Three soldiers enter the house with rifles leveled at the occupants.

"Don't shoot. We are not armed!" Father shouts to the corporal in charge.

"Then why did you not open the door as I ordered?" says the burly soldier wearing a soiled uniform and gives the appearance of one who was hardened by battle.

We apologize, sir. I was about to change the little girl's diaper," my mother answers. "Evidently, she's made quite a mess."

The corporal is skeptical but moves on to the reason for the intrusion. "We heard reports that you have an infant son. Is this true?"

"No, just the baby girl."

"Then you shouldn't mind if we look around," the man demands and signals his two comrades to do a search. My parents, Osigian and Mary Nighosian, nervously wait as the soldiers check each room. The corporal remains with the parents, but his eyes are focused on the baby.

"Hmm, such an odd-looking child, but then I could say that about all Armenians," he says and launches a wad of spit onto the floor.

The soldiers return to report finding no other occupants and begin to exit the house, but something has raised the corporal's curiosity. He approaches the crib. My parents fear at any moment he will discover they are hiding a son. Concern for their child's safety prompts my mother to make a dangerous decision.

"Perhaps you would care to assist me," she says, handing the corporal a clean diaper. Then she picks up her baby and mocks smelling a stench. "Whew, this child has really filled her underpants this time!" she says, waving her hand back and forth pretending to clear the air. The ploy works and the corporal backs away, but he still has suspicions.

The other soldiers grow impatient when they see the man is determined to peek under the baby's smock. My father cannot allow that to happen even if it means risking his life to save his child. Before he can act, the other soldiers unknowingly intervene on behalf of the Armenian family. They are accustomed to their corporal's unsavory quirks.

"So now you have sunk so low that you must look at the little girl's parts," one soldier chastises. "We always thought you were a little strange, Asid." The two soldiers burst into laughter, but the corporal is not amused by the embarrassing comment. He quickly withdraws his fingers from the smock. The baby's gender remains concealed, and the man turns his attention to the head of our household.

"I will keep my eyes on you Osigian Nighosian. You may be one of the Armenians making trouble for us."

The soldier has no idea just how right he is...

Note: Noah's Ark came to rest after the Great Flood on Mount Ararat in ancient Armenia. Armenians are believed to be descendants of Hayk, the great, great grandson of Noah. (National Geographic: The Rebirth of Armenia)

Chapter 2

1915

"Good morning, my handsome son." Mother's greeting brings happiness to my heart as I enter our kitchen savoring the aroma of baked choreg. She is a wonderful cook and her sweetbread is favored in our home. "Your uncles Ara and Varge will join us to help with work at the farm a few miles from the village."

It is welcomed news, but I am more interested in the usual guest seated at the kitchen table. Our friendly neighbor, Arixie Enjaian, holds her infant daughter while sipping coffee from a small porcelain cup. Her two-year old son plays on the floor.

Arixie's brothers, Abraham and Yesa, live with her and help care for the two children. She and the two brothers arrived in Amasia years ago when her village was invaded by Ottoman soldiers. Her husband died earlier during a battle to protect another Armenian village.

I refer to Arixie as my *morakooeer*, although she is not a true aunt. It is not uncommon for good friends to become extended family, aunts and uncles to Armenian children. She visits each morning to have coffee and chat with my mother.

"Parev Nishan. Eench bes ek?" (Hello, Nishan. How are you?) Her broad smile is accompanied with a hug.

"Shad lav." (Very well.) I reply in Armenian because the older generation believes it is important to maintain the language now that our nation has been overrun by Turks and Kurds. I am too young to grasp the political ramifications of losing one's national identity.

Arixie gives a pleasing nod and returns to sipping the strong black coffee from her demitasse cup. She always leaves a few drops at the bottom to turn the cup upside down for the drippings to form a pattern inside the cup. Then, with a quick flick of her wrist, the cup is returned to an upright position whereupon she endeavors to predict my future. It is a custom that helps bond Armenian children with the older generation. I find it exciting; the predictions are always filled with joyous thoughts.

This is a special day. After spending time playing with friends, I will join my family for the trip to our small orchard and garden plot. Two family members will be privileged to ride donkeys to the location while others make the journey on foot. If I am lucky, an uncle will boost me onto one of the animals. The orchard should be abundant with pomegranates, olives, figs, and apricots this time of the year. We also tend to fields that produce vegetables and grain crops. Our people are good farmers who respect the land.

My enthusiasm is tempered by fear of the Turkish soldiers who patrol our land. Their hatred for the Armenians is evidenced by many recent gravesites. There is danger in every encounter with the Turks, especially for my father. He is the lieutenant governor of our village, but that ranking position is a double-edged sword. Turkish government officials in Constantinople know they must effectively interact with my father to present a false sense of cordial Armenian/Turkish relations to other nations. What the Turks do not know is that he lives another life as a freedom-fighter engaged in armed combat to protect the Armenian people. I am anxious to see my father today when he returns to Amasia. His absence from our home the past three days is said to be for political purposes, but I believe he is on an assignment as a soldier of Armenia. I worry that he could meet the same fate as Arixie's husband. Today, I listen intently as she vividly describes the battle.

"The year was 1904. My husband was one of 200 soldiers in the Armenian Revolutionary Federation. They were sent to the area of Sassoun to protect civilians from the plundering and killings by the Kurds. Our men encountered a massive force of 15,000 Ottoman and Kurdish troops. The enemy was supported by mountain cannons and machine guns. The Armenian soldiers fought bravely for days but only a few survived. Eventually, the victors entered many villages and committed many terrible atrocities. They raped women, beheaded our men, and even the children were not spared from the sword. Then, when the Allied countries tried to intervene, Germany helped Turkey gloss over the massacres."

"That is enough storytelling for one day. Young ears need not hear such doom and gloom," Mother says. She nods in my direction and gives a stern frown to our neighbor. Arixie has been allowed to reminisce out of friendship, but it is time to end it.

"Why not, Mary? How else will future generations learn the truth about a genocide that threatens to wipe out an entire nation?" Arixie asks, to counter my mother's opinion.

Mother has no interest in carrying on a political debate this early in the morning. She avoids the discussion and turns her attention elsewhere. "Nishan, you can play outside until we leave," she tells me, "and share these with your friends." She places three pieces of warm choreg in my hands and gives me a hug. My older friends, Zaven and Aram, most likely are waiting to engage me in a game of shooting marbles.

Before leaving, I ask Arixie to gaze into her cup to tell my fortune. She glances to my mother for approval and then motions for me to sit beside her. The ritual of flipping the cup is completed, and the insides are covered in dark patterns of thick coffee residue.

"A-ha! You are such a fortunate person!" Arixie bursts with enthusiasm while keeping her eyes fixed on the streams of drippings. "I see you entertaining your friends and getting many gifts for birthday number eight. It is only a matter of weeks." I give her a hug as she continues to look in the cup. "I also see you becoming a prosperous young man, perhaps a rich merchant or even a doctor." My mother listens with an appeasing smile for her neighbor friend. "Oh, my goodness, can it be? Yes, Nishan, there is a beautiful bride and many children in your future." The women laugh as an embarrassing blush spreads across my face. The session comes to an end, and I am given permission to leave the table. Arixie plants a kiss on my cheek and confirms that I need never wonder about her feelings for me. "Nishan, you are a good boy and I love you."

"Thank you, Arixie; I love you, too."

I hurriedly start for the front door when Mother admonishes, "Be very careful, my son. The soldiers on daily patrol will come through the village. They always look for an excuse to harm our people." Her soft lips brush my cheek as she whispers, "I love you, Nishan."

Note: In the 1st century, Disciples of Christ, Bartholomew and Thaddeus bring Christianity to Armenia. In 301 A.D., Saint Gregory converts the Armenian king, Tiridates. Armenia becomes the first nation in the world to proclaim Christianity as its national religion. (Wikipedia: Armenia's Conversion to Christianity)

Chapter 3

"Well, it's about time!" Zaven and Aram shout in unison when they see me exit the house carrying fresh-baked sweetbreads cradled in my arm.

"You are slower than the Turkish sergeant who leads the soldiers through our streets each day," Aram chides and punches my arm hard enough to spill the choreg on the ground. He knows that I detest the comparison with our nemesis, the obese and scarred Sgt. Asid who constantly abuses the citizens of Amasia. Yes, he is the same soldier my parents mention when they recall the incident in our home years ago that could have ended my life. The years have given him a higher rank and he remains an evil person. An Armenian sword many battles earlier took one of his eyes and gave him a jagged scar slicing across his hooked nose. The distorted face is a grotesque reminder of the savagery associated with the invasion of our country.

"Leave him alone," Zaven yells and pushes Aram aside. "Pick on someone your own size." His flexed arm reveals a well-exercised bicep that Aram declines to challenge. Zaven kneels to help me retrieve the fallen bread. "Don't mind him. Sometimes his brain doesn't work right, but he's really a good fellow."

I like Zaven Monoogian. He is four years older and quite protective of me. Perhaps it is because

Zaven lost his family in 1909 while he was visiting relatives in Amasia. His father and mother were merchants in the town of Adana when relations between the Christian Armenians and Muslins turned to armed conflict. Many Armenians were killed including my friend's parents. His trip to our village most likely saved him from being listed among those who perished. I was with Zaven when his uncle in Amasia reported that the death toll rose to nearly 30,000 men, women, and children who died during the siege; many of them burned to death while seeking refuge in churches. I think Zaven treats me like a younger brother now that there's only his aunt and uncle living in Amasia.

"Are we going to shoot marbles or talk all day?" Aram's irritated tone puts an end to our small talk. I proceed to share the choreg with each friend. It is quickly devoured, and Aram pats his stomach. "My goodness, your mother is a fantastic cook! Next time tell her to prepare shish kebabs for us." He smiled. The three of us have a good laugh as we walk to a patch of soft dirt under an olive tree. Zaven retrieves a fallen twig and scratches a circle the size of a small wagon wheel in the loose earth. It's time to get down to the business of winning each other's marbles.

The small balls are not actually marbles. They are round cylinders which once served as the caps for bottles of soda water sent from organizations in countries that are sympathetic to the Armenians. The donation of liquid, food, blankets, and other supplies is welcomed throughout our region since the Ottoman government has confiscated increasing amounts of what we produce. Mother tells me that parents in other nations encourage their children not to waste the food on their dinner plates and to "remember the starving Armenians." The international gesture is appreciated, but sadly it falls short of our need for weapons and ammunition to resist the invaders. I am still a child and fail to comprehend the magnitude of worldly conflict. Today, my battle is against a foe that has more marbles.

My six marbles have been salvaged from soda bottles over a period of four weeks. The procedure is simple. I peel the wax coating from the round cap on a full bottle. Then, using the palm of my hand, I tap the ball and drive it through the narrow opening of the neck until it drops inside the bottle. Once the liquid is consumed, I shatter the glass bottle against the ground and retrieve the marble.

Zaven, Aram, and I put an equal number of marbles in the center of the dirt circle. We each keep our favorite one to use as a taw, the shooter ball.

"I will take the first shot; then we can see what Aram can do," Zaven announces.

"Hey, that's not fair. Why do I always have to be last?" My objection receives a terse reply.

"Because I'm the oldest and wisest," Zaven replies, raising his eyebrows to indicate he's heard the objection many times. It is true; both friends are older, and our time for play together is shorter than

I realize. He crouches on the ground with his thumb and forefinger around his best marble. An exaggerated squint makes him appear as a sniper bent on eliminating an enemy. A flick of his thumb launches the round missile. It briefly takes flight and then lands on the ground rolling a straight path through the dirt until it smashes into the small balls assembled in the center of the tiny arena. The glass spheres fly in all directions like a meteor burst.

"Three for me!" Zaven shouts as he gathers the marbles that landed beyond the perimeter. Aram and I aren't nearly as jubilant. One of the captured balls belongs to Aram; the other two are mine. Zaven has earned the right to continue shooting unless he fails to knock out any more balls. Such is not the case, and his precision shots quickly void the ring of every ball. In moments, the small treasures that took weeks to acquire are no longer in my possession.

"Well, that sure didn't take long," Aram grumbles but doesn't seem bothered by the loss of a few round balls. I am not as accepting of the loss and my disappointment does not go unnoticed.

"Nishan, why look so sad?" Zaven asks. I lower my head so as not to draw attention to the tear about to drip from my eye. My friend attempts to rationalize the matter with a series of exclamations accompanied by erratic waves of his hand. "Be cheerful, my friend! You should be happy for me! Rejoice! We are Armenians!" The exaggerated show of affection brings a smile to my face. I wipe away the tear and become amused as Aram rolls on the ground trying to contain his laughter over Zaven's antics. There is more joy when my friend places his newly-acquired marbles into the palm of my hand and whispers, "Keep the marbles, Nishan, and always remember the good times we have shared together."

"What about me? Don't I get my marbles back?" Aram pleads for equal treatment. Zaven's response is to the point.

"No, you don't. You're old enough to know better than to play against me. If you're that stupid, you deserve to lose." He plops Aram's marbles into a pouch and gives me a satisfied wink. For the next few minutes, Aram decides to sketch figures in the soft dirt with the stick we used to make the circle. It gives Zaven time to take me aside for a private lesson with marbles.

"Nishan, if you are ever going to get good with marbles, you need to learn a trick about shooting," he tells me. "Watch me and learn, my young friend." This excites me. Zaven is going to show me just how he manages to accumulate such a large cache of marbles from the youth of Amasia.

"Watch closely," my friend says, dropping to his knees and spreading two marbles on the ground. "It doesn't really matter which marble you use as the taw because it's how you do the shot that counts." He selects one of the marbles and grips it between his thumb and forefinger. One eye is closed and the other one squints as he leans forward. "Now, watch my thumb as I launch the taw." Sure enough, when Zaven fires the marble, it flies three or four inches until touching the ground and traveling on a rapid course. It picks up momentum until smashing into the other marble and knocking it outside the circle.

"Wow! Great shot!" My excited yell is followed by a congratulatory pat on Zaven's back. Aram looks up from his sketching but does not appear to be impressed. Evidently, he has witnessed the shot on numerous occasions that caused him to hand over his marbles to the better player. Zaven keeps his attention on me.

"So, you see, Nishan, the secret is to not have the dirt slow down the marble. If you take good aim and fire it into the air just right, the marble will pick up speed when it hits the ground. Practice, my friend, and you will win marbles."

"I will." I appreciate Zaven's lesson, but not nearly as much as his friendship.

Mother has not called for me to join the family for our journey, so we decide to play a different game. Aram produces a small knife from the back pocket of his *shalwar*. The baggy trousers always hang loosely on his hips. I wonder if the tattered rope tied around his waist will someday give way and expose more of Aram than I care to see. The new game centers on who can toss the knife closest to a mark on the ground, but shortly after beginning, a threatening voice grabs our attention. Turkish soldiers have arrived being led by the evil Sgt. Asid. The fun and games come to an end.

Note: The first war for religious freedom is fought in 451 A.D. when the Armenian people valiantly fight the armies of Persia, refusing to accept Zorastrianism and cling to their Christian faith. This brave stand for Chrisitanity is still celebrated by Armenians today. (Susie Hoogasian-Villa: 100 Armenian Tales)

Chapter 4

"Well, what do we have here? Three pups fathered by Armenian dogs of the land." The sound of Sgt. Asid's voice makes my skin crawl. He and his troops are known for their abuse of our people. The foot soldiers encircle us to prevent escape as their leader clumsily dismounts a weary horse.

He squats to retrieve Aram's knife. "Is this a weapon you intend to use against the soldiers of the Ottoman Empire?" It is an absurd notion, but the implication is obvious to me. Months earlier and fearing a reprisal for travesties conducted against our people, the Turkish regime ordered its troops to disarm the entire Armenian population of the region. Persons found to harbor weapons are now imprisoned or simply disappear, never to be heard from again. I am afraid, and the disfigured sergeant is relentless in his nastiness. He pulls Aram closer and presses the knife against our friend's neck.

"See how easily I could execute this Armenian pup for having this weapon," he tells his men. The soldiers appease their sergeant with laughter, knowing that to remain silent could easily bring them an equal fate. Aram squirms to get away, but the cruel man retains a death grip on his throat.

"Leave him alone, you Turkish pig!" Zaven's outburst draws the attention of the soldiers and the ire of their leader. He starts toward the sergeant, but several rifle bayonets halt the advance. Thus far, the sergeant has been fixed on Aram, but now his attention is squarely on someone he recognizes. "My goodness, who can this be?" Sergeant Asid uses a meaty hand to clutch my friend's chin and carefully examines Zaven's features. "Well, if it isn't the orphaned Manoogian boy." He remains silent. His disdain for the gnarled man is obvious. "It's too bad you weren't with your parents at Adana. We could be rid of the entire family." The vile remark is a cruel reminder that the sergeant participated in slaughtering the citizens of Adana. "You bastard! I will kill you!" Zaven's attempt to charge the man is met by the hard blow from a soldier's rifle butt and he slumps to the dirt. Aram rushes to restrain our friend, fearing that another attempt will end in tragedy for all of us. I am unable to aid either of my friends. This cruelty is something I have only heard about, but the blood flowing from Zaven's forehead is very real. Now the sergeant is coming toward me, and I no longer worry about the others for I am his next victim.

"Praise Alla! I have caught two little fish in one day," Sgt. Asid cries out to his men when he recognizes me. He has been in my parents' home on more than one occasion to summon my father for meetings with Turkish officials. "Are you not the Nighosian boy?" My eyes are focused on the ground, so he raises my chin and leans forward to study my features.

"Yes, I know you," he says, rubbing the ugly scar across his face. "Your father served with General Antranik at the battle of Adana. He was lucky to survive, but there will be another time for him to feel my blade!" I am close enough to the hideous gash that distorts half his face. Many weathered stitches reconnect a piece of his nostril and eye brow which appears to have been nearly sliced off. I am sure his hands feel my body shuddering as I respond to the question.

"Yes, sir." I meekly own up to my family name. "I am Nishan Nighosian." I try to be brave, but the stench from his body and soiled uniform is overwhelming. Beads of sweat dripping off his beard onto my clothes make me nauseous. Turning my head aside only brings forth more agitation from my captor.

"Look at me when I talk to you!" The hateful command is accompanied by a blast of spittle onto my face. My eyes are squeezed shut, but I feel and smell the pungent spray. The sergeant doubles his fist and prepares to deliver a blow. I am now in a precarious position; even my father's influence as a community leader cannot help me.

"Touch him again and you will pay dearly," Zaven yells. "Your superiors in Constantinople will cut off your head if you harm the boy."

Turkish leaders are increasingly suspicious that Armenian officials such as my father are developing closer ties to neighboring Russia. However, they still need our people to further Ottoman interests in matters of commerce and international affairs. The punishment for a soldier who disrupts that sensitive alliance would be death. The sergeant strokes the curls of his beard and contemplates the options. An anguished grimace stretches his neck muscles, but my friend's admonishment is effective and brings a halt to the attack. Once again, Zaven comes to my rescue and puts an end to the harassment. The sergeant releases me, but a hateful sneer tells me that I have made an enemy for life.

There seems to be unrest among the soldiers who have witnessed a weakness demonstrated by their leader. Sgt. Asid mounts his horse and makes a pronouncement to establish order. It is directed to three Armenian boys but the message is intended for an entire nation.

"You silly people. There will come a time when you will no longer be useful to the Ottoman Empire. Then the new leaders will order their soldiers to take your properties and be done with you!" I understand the message.

In 1908, a group known as Young Turks successfully deposed the Sultan of Turkey. At the time, my father thought it might promote improved relations among various ethnic groups, but that has not proven to be the case. The Turks seem to hate us regardless of whether or not we appear to be a part of either regime.

I am relieved the soldiers are departing, but the sergeant cannot restrain his hatefulness as he rides past Zaven. "Be very careful how you treat your masters, or you will suffer the same fate as your family in Adana."

Zaven remains silent even when Sgt. Asid strikes him across the face with the handle of his horse whip. The soldiers are surprised that my friend remains solemn despite the severe blow. They quickly fall into formation and march down the street behind their mounted leader.

"Are you okay, Zaven?"

"Yes, Nishan. The hurt is in my heart and not my face." He uses his shirt sleeve to wipe blood oozing from the cut on his cheek. When I comment about the red stain left on his shirt, his response seems more like a prophecy, "Never mind, Nishan. A stain will eventually wash away, but sadness in one's heart remains forever."

"My parents are going to be really upset about this," Aram chimes in. "They probably won't let me be outside for some time."

"Tell your parents nothing. It will only cause trouble for them if they try to retaliate. That goes for both of you," Zaven advises.

"I am afraid my father will find out anyway," I tell both friends. "The sergeant has been to my house and he may return." Sharing the concern does little to alleviate my fear, especially when Zaven ends the conversation with a prediction.

"I wouldn't worry about it, Nishan. The Turk may not live long enough to harm another person."

His words are on my mind as I rush home to be with my family to harvest produce. I am unaware that my two friends will spend their afternoon planning an assassination.

Note: During 1876 to 1909, Abdul Hamid II rules as the last Sultan of the Ottoman Empire. During his reign, thousands of Christian Armenians are slaughtered. The attempted genocide prompts allied nations to label him "The Bloody Sultan." (Wikipedia: The Bloody Sultan)

Chapter 5

My father arrives home in time to join us for the trek to our farm located four miles from the village. I am happy to see him and curious about his absence.

"Father, I have missed you. Where have you been?" His response is terse, almost programmed.

"Official business, my prince. It is nothing for you to worry about." I am curious about the endearing term. It is not the first time he has used it when referring to me. My questioning look receives a casual response. "Someday you will understand."

He is weary from his travels and gives me a welcomed hug. A pleasant smile tells me I am loved. My suspicion that he has completed a dangerous mission is confirmed when I observe him stash a pistol, rifle, and bandoleer of bullets into a hiding place.

Our journey along the winding path to the farm takes nearly an hour. We travel through a small forest and over rough terrain. Uncles Ara and Varge lead donkeys strapped with pouches of water and large baskets which will hold fruits and vegetables on the return trip. I am the youngest and fortunate to hitch a ride on one of the animals. Knowing my days of being treated as a child will end soon, I enjoy every minute of it. I understand I will join the others in traveling on foot before long.

Arixie Enjaian accompanies us, although her thoughts remain with the baby daughter and son who are being cared for by a neighboring couple in Amasia.

The workload is divided upon arrival at our destination. My father and uncles tend to a small grove of olive, fig, and apricot trees. Mother and Arixie work in the garden containing vegetables such as potatoes, turnips, beets, and okra. I am assigned to provide water to each person and the animals. It is menial work, but Mother reassures me it is vital to our mission.

"If we suffer from thirst, we cannot harvest the food to share with the people of our village. Yes, Nishan, you have a most important job." Her encouragement brings renewed vigor to my work.

It is mid-afternoon when we pause to eat. A woolen blanket is used to display an assortment of boregs that Mother has prepared for the journey. They are delicious cheese turnovers. Arixie becomes the most popular person in the group when she brings forth a batch of crescent cookies. The nut and raisin-filled pastries sprinkled with sugar are a special treat, especially with the current necessity to ration food. This generosity has cost her a full week's supply of cooking ingredients. When praised for her thoughtfulness, she pats her tummy and modestly replies, "Perhaps I needed to lose a few pounds anyway."

Father and I seize the opportunity to rest on a boulder. He does not speak and continually gazes into the sky. My curiosity is aroused. "Father, what are you looking for?"

His response is thought-provoking, almost mystical. "I seek guidance from the Lord, my son. That is why I turn to the Mountain of Noah." There is no elaboration as he continues to stare toward an unseen mountain.

I am bewildered by the comment, but I have some knowledge of the place he mentions. Our people believe this mountain is blessed by the Lord. "Father, I am confused. What do you find in the mountain?"

"The Mountain of Noah is sacred. I cannot see it, but I know it exists. That is what we call faith." I know my father is sharing something important, so I listen carefully. "That mountain and our abiding faith is a legacy passed down by generations of our people. We were the first to establish Christianity as our national religion. That is one reason why the Turks, Kurds, and others have hated us for centuries. You, my prince, are part of that legacy." His choice of words captures my attention once again.

"Father, we are not royalty. We do not live in a palace. Why do you continue to call me a prince?"

"We will talk about it at the appropriate time," he said after pausing for a moment to reflect on the question. "Right now, we should return to work. Please notify the others."

There is no further mention of our conversation the rest of the afternoon. Mother and Arixie eliminate weeds in the garden and fill two huge baskets with vegetables. The men carefully prune dead wood from the orchard trees. They harvest what fruit has ripened. Eventually, four large baskets laden with produce are lashed onto the donkeys. There will be no riders on the return trip to Amasia, but no one seems to mind. It is a productive afternoon and we are pleased that our village will benefit from it.

~~~~~~~~~~~~~~~~~~~~~~~~~~

It is only when we are halfway home that danger approaches. Five men on horseback block the trail as we travel through a clump of timber. Father and my uncles come to the forefront to engage the men.

"Please allow us to pass," he asks in a firm voice. A leader for the band of soldiers recognizes him.

"And, if we don't Mr. Neghosian? Will you throw apricots and okra at us?" The offensive comment brings laughter from the horsemen who wear a different uniform from their leader. The man issuing the challenge remains fixed on my father while his hand rests on a sidearm. Mother positions herself in front of me, as Father gives instructions to everyone in a low voice so as not to be overheard by our intimidators.

"Everyone, remain calm; do not antagonize them. The four men wearing the long coats are Hamidiyehs, most likely Kurdish tribesmen that are recruited by the Turks to raid our villages." He continues to assess the situation and nods toward the leader. "That one is a Turkish officer assigned to this band of thieves and murderers."

Our men are outnumbered. The few knives we brought for work are no match for a rifle or sword carried by each Hamidiyeh soldier. Arixie comes closer and billows her peasant dress until it engulfs me like a tent. I can no longer see the men on horseback from my hiding spot. I fear that the confrontation is about to become a battle, but then my mother responds to the leader's sarcastic question.

"We would not think of wasting perfectly good fruit and vegetables when it is so much better to share." Mother's appeasing words catch everyone by surprise. I peek from behind Arixie's dress and see the soldiers giving odd looks to one another. "We will be pleased to give half of our yield to such brave men who protect our village." My father is not pleased with Mother's false flattery, but he understands her wisdom and remains silent.

The Turkish officer sees an opportunity. After all, it may not be wise to slaughter the family of a village official who has the attention of powerful people in the capital city. He orders two soldiers to dismount and retrieve one of the huge baskets. We all think the tense encounter may be resolved, but our relief is premature.

"Wait! Leave the baskets that are strapped to the animal," the officer commands. "Bring the donkey, too."

I fear my father will launch an attack, but Mother's firm grip on his shoulder gives him cause to consider the consequences, so he holds fast. We watch the thieves ride past us. The donkey and half of our hard work vanish in a matter of seconds. For a second time in one day, I am exposed to the cruelty of people toward one another due to hatred and greed.

Our journey home is somber but without further incident. Now, even I look toward Mount Ararat and wonder: *If we are people chosen by the Savior, then why are we treated so poorly?*

Note: In 1893, Armenian women who refuse to forsake Christianity and adopt Islam are locked in churches and put to death. Armenian children are lined up one behind the other as Turkish soldiers see how many heads a bullet can pass through. (Armenian Massacres and Turkish Tyranny)

Chapter 6

There is little daylight remaining by the time we arrive at the village. Mother excuses me to seek out my friends as she and the others distribute what remains of today's harvest. Word of the encounter with the Himidiyeh raiders quickly spreads along the streets. I locate Zaven and Aram at our usual meeting spot. They patiently listen to my account of the incident on the trail, but it is obvious they have something more important on their minds.

"Nishan, we have something to tell you if you can keep a secret." I give the needed assurance and Zaven proceeds to tell me they have hatched a plot to kill Sgt. Asid. I think the two friends are just fooling with me, but I soon realize they are serious about their plan when each one displays a sturdy spear carved from fallen limbs. The weapons are crude but could kill.

"If yours doesn't get him, mine surely will." Aram makes several jabs with his spear as though he's challenging an enemy. Zaven is not amused.

"That's not a toy," he says, putting a halt to the playfulness. "Put it away now! We've got plans to make."

During the next several minutes, I am given a hasty rundown of what the two adolescents were up to all afternoon. They speak of hiking to a natural rock formation on the outskirts of Amasia that appears to be a good spot for an ambush. The soldiers on patrol must circle the mass of stone on their approach to the village. The location is unique due to its many caverns. There is even a small tunnel running the entire length in one of the secluded caves. We call it our secret place because the highest ceiling is barely three feet from the floor. The tunnel is too low to be of any use for adults who wish to save a quarter-mile hike around this huge assemblage of volcanic rock. Neither Aram nor I have ever gone more than thirty feet inside the narrow passageway, but Zaven tells us he made it all the way from one end to the other by crawling on his knees. The distance through the tunnel is not the main issue, but cramped quarters, little light, and crumbling rock increase the danger. I feel intense fear for my two friends.

"So, that's your plan? You are going to crawl with spears through a small tunnel for two hundred feet, ambush a patrol, and stab the leader to death with sharpened limbs?" The sarcasm receives a hasty response.

"The soldiers are always far behind and on foot. By the time the sergeant realizes what's happening, we will have speared him off the horse," Aram informs me. He anticipates my next question and explains further. "And, yes, if the soldiers do pursue us, they'll be stopped when the tunnel narrows to just a crawl space."

There is grave danger in this foolhardy plan. I should end my involvement right now, but a sense of adventure comes over me. "Do I get a spear, too?"

"No, you don't even get to throw a rock, but you can help us," Zaven tells me. I eagerly listen to my assignment. "This is no game, Nishan. You must promise to follow my instructions and never place yourself in danger." He adds an afterthought. "My young friend, that means even if I fail to return. Do you make the promise?"

"Yes, Zaven, I promise."

Based on the commitment, he tells me that I will be a lookout stationed high on the rock formation. It gives me not only a full view of the approaching soldiers, but also, I will see the location where my friends will enter the tunnel.

"From your vantage point, Nishan, you will be able to see everything that happens. You can signal us if anything does not appear to be right as the soldiers approach the point of attack." He hands me a long scarf that shields his face from dust. "Use this as a signal and keep it. After all, you are my trusted friend."

Note: Clara Barton, founder of the American Red Cross, arrives in Constantinople on February 16, 1896 with a relief expedition to provide medical aid to the suffering and starving Armenians. Turkish government officials try to sabotage the relief effort. (Wikipedia: Armenian Mission/Angel of the Battlefield)

Chapter 7

"Make sure you stay clear of the soldiers if you're going to be outside today," Mother cautions me in the morning. The promise to Zaven about staying out of danger reinforces her directive. I kiss her cheek and head for the rendezvous spot near the road entering our village.

"Late again, I see." Aram's criticism is expected even though he knows I have chores to do each morning. Zaven ignores the comment and gives me a hug.

"Ah, my friend, you joined us on this glorious day!" He gives a pat on my back for encouragement. "Never mind the idiot," he says, nodding toward Aram. "He's just nervous and probably afraid the fat Turk will sit on him if he misses with the spear." Zaven's comment draws my attention to the modified pieces of wood each friend holds. The crude weapons look even sharper than on the previous evening, no doubt having been honed to inflict the maximum penetration. "Come; let me take you to your post."

Aram waits by the narrow opening at the foot of the rock formation while Zaven and I make the climb to the top. The front elevation facing the road is steep, but our access on the sloped backside is more accessible.

"I can see for many miles from up here. There shouldn't be any problem giving you the signal," I say, clutching the scarf Zaven has given me. "You can count on me." My expression of confidence draws a repeated lecture.

"I'm sure we can, but I am more interested in your promise. Remember, under no circumstances are you to expose yourself to danger. I put my faith in you." His kind statement seals my commitment to helping them.

The next hour is tedious as I anxiously watch for the Turkish patrol. My perch on the craggy rocks is at least eighty feet above the road. I will have ample time to warn Aram and Zaven of the approaching troops. Upon seeing the signal, my friends will drop to their knees and crawl through the tunnel. The ambush will take place close to where they exit. Once the sergeant is killed, they will scramble back to safety through the tunnel. The patrol of bewildered soldiers will fail in trying to negotiate a hole barely half their size.

I gaze at the item given to me before my friend left to pursue this dangerous mission. It is just a peasant scarf, but it holds great sentimental value for me. Zaven has no wealth, and yet he shared one of his few possessions. He truly is a special friend.

The plan sounded simple enough when we talked about it the previous day. Now my thoughts worry me: *The sergeant has brazenly ridden his horse ahead of his troops on prior occasions. The purpose of this bravado was most likely to impress his soldiers that he has no fear of the villagers. I now realize that my friends are doomed if the distance between the marching men and their leader is not great enough. I think we should abandon this plan and return to our homes. We are still boys; war is for men.*

It's too late. There is movement on the road. My eyes cannot mistake the large figure on horseback. His soldiers have difficulty keeping pace and have fallen behind. When their leader rounds the bend in the road, they temporarily will lose sight of him. My friends must strike at that precise moment, but first I must do my part. I wave the scarf entrusted to me and it immediately draws attention. Zaven gives an acknowledgement. My two friends enter the tunnel that will take them through the massive stone. I have fulfilled my assignment. If my companions are successful, we will have struck a blow for the Armenian people.

I nervously shift my eyes back and forth between the approaching formation and the spot where the tunnel ends. It seems my companions are taking a long time traversing the entire length of the narrow cavern, but it is less than two minutes until I catch a glimpse of movement. Zaven and Aram are now hiding in shrubs growing along the road. My high vantage point affords the opportunity to see the action unfold. The mounted sergeant is only a short distance from rounding the bend. His well-armed escort will soon lose sight of him. My friends are preparing to launch their spears. Anticipation of the impending strike is playing havoc with my emotions. I even feel sad for the panting beast that labors under the heavy weight of one who is soon to be executed. The scene plays out as Zaven described it. I am about to witness my first battle for the Ottoman Empire, even though it is only between one Turkish soldier and two Armenian boys. The moment is here.

This day is a turning point in my life as the joy of a fantasy is dashed and replaced with the reality of life. Today, something bad will happen.

Zaven and Aram spring from the hiding place bent on impaling Sgt. Asid. He reacts but has difficulty drawing his pistol while trying to maintain control of the startled mount. The horse rears its front legs when challenged by the spears and bucks the rider onto the ground. Aram seizes an opportunity and sends his spear flying, but it misses the mark and sails over the dazed sergeant's head. A defenseless Aram quickly retreats to the tunnel. Zaven has advanced and is now close enough to jab his spear into the man's midsection. He lunges forward and feels the sharp point sink into a mass of loose flesh. Sgt. Asid clutches the embedded wood with both hands. Earlier, I imagined seeing a man lying on the ground taking his final breath, but this is different. I can hear his screams even this far from the encounter. "Come quickly! Help me!"

Zaven must be as surprised as I am. He stands staring at the pained human struggling with the protruding wood in his belly. There are only seconds before the soldiers will have Zaven in their sights. He takes hold of the opposite end of the spear and attempts to drive it deeper into the wailing human. The man pushes back and now both are engaged in a death struggle for control of the spear. Several soldiers approaching hesitate to shoot for fear of hitting their leader. Zaven's only hope is to escape to the tunnel, but that exposes him as a target. He is out of time. The soldiers are taking deadly aim.

Aram is safely into the hole, but Zaven has no chance to reach the opening before being felled by a hail of bullets. I am his only hope for survival, so I begin throwing rocks from my position on the cliff. In fearing for my friend's life, I break my promise to him.

The wild flinging of anything I can grasp in my hands causes enough distraction to give my friend the precious seconds he needs. The soldiers cover their heads from the pellets of stone. Zaven disappears into the crevice, but now the soldiers are aware that a third youth is involved in the attack. More disappointment comes when I see Sgt. Asid is successful in casting aside the spear which has failed to inflict a mortal wound. Soldiers are now helping the wounded man to his feet.

I believe Aram and Zaven are now scrambling on their knees through the tunnel, so I hurry to the opposite end of my perch hoping to see them emerge. When they appear, I will shuffle down the slope to join them in the escape. Even if the soldiers try to continue their pursuit through the tunnel, they will be halted at a spot where the clearance narrows to just enough space for an agile youth.

I continue to scan the ground below knowing that at any moment I should see movement. Sure enough, Aram appears and doesn't hesitate to sprint toward a knoll for seclusion. Next is Zaven on his belly, shifting his weight back and forth to squeeze through the entrance hole. I am filled with joy, especially when he waves to me before heading for the knoll to join Aram. I begin my descent and keep my eyes focused on Zaven sprinting to safety. Then, muffled shots echo out of nowhere. There is not a soldier in sight, but the bullet hits its target. Zaven lurches to the ground and remains still. I see blood staining the back of his head and realize that the wound is fatal. One of the pursuing soldiers, having been stopped at the narrow end of the tunnel, must have fired the shot from a prone position. I have lost a dear friend and any childhood innocence I had left.

The soldiers appear to be more concerned with the two boys who attacked the sergeant than the person who threw rocks at them. A few examine Zaven's lifeless body while others search the countryside for Aram. In all the commotion, I make my escape from the rock formation. Later, I sheepishly enter my home without saying a word about the tragic event. The night is filled with tears for a lost friend and an intense fear that a knock on the front door will doom my entire family.

Note: Conflict between Armenians and the Turks was not only focused on religious beliefs. The Turks wanted trade routes which passed through Armenia. They were also jealous that Armenians were successful in various walks of life; business, industry, finance, agriculture, textiles, politics, etc.

(Armenian Massacres and Turkish Tyranny)

Chapter 8

By morning news of the ambush spreads quickly through the village. I listen from the hallway to hear a conversation coming from the kitchen.

"The sergeant wasn't badly wounded, but the Turks are irate over the incident," my father relates to the two women having their morning coffee. "There will be retribution for sure."

"Is it not enough that they have the blood of death on their hands?" Arixie Enjaian angrily cries out. "They murdered a child!"

"There is no exception for age when the infidels choose to slaughter," my father responds in a somber tone. Mother remains silent. I wonder if she suspects that my activity on the previous afternoon was not mere child's play.

"It will not be safe on the streets," Father warns. "Keep the boy in the house. If they come, do nothing to incite them. They will use any excuse to justify their actions." I quietly step closer to peek into the kitchen. Father looks weary as though he has not slept. Perhaps he spent the night conversing with other men in the village. "We will know the village is targeted for an invasion if Constantinople sends more troops into the region. Our men will fight to stop them before they enter Amasia."

"We should fear for our young men," Arixie interjects to the conversation. "My brothers, Abraham and Yesa, have done nothing to be put in this position of fearing for their lives."

"You are wrong, Arixie," Mother says to set the record straight. "If the Turks invade Amasia, no one in the region is safe. Men, women, and children will feel the razor edge of their swords just as they did in Sasson, Adana, Caesarea, Malatya, and so many other communities. No one will be spared." She bows her head and murmurs a prayer.

I notice Arixie turn her cup over onto the saucer, an indication she is about to make a prediction. Her usual smile turns to a frown when the cup is returned to an upright position. The furrowed brow reflects a worried lady.

"What do the coffee drippings tell you, Arixie?" my father asks. There is not an immediate reply. Our neighbor lady is troubled and hesitant to speak.

"Come now, Arixie, surely the coffee wasn't that bad," Father muses. The attempt to lighten the mood does not produce the desired result.

When the bewildered lady finally speaks, her words come forth steeped with emotion. "I see darkness and destruction in our future," she bemoans. "There is great suffering for our people and much sadness for many lost souls."

"Enough of this doom and gloom." Father's usual calm demeanor is gone as he makes a stern pronouncement. "The Armenian people will put their future in the hands of God and not some cup stained with Turkish coffee!"

I am frightened by his outburst. *Did our actions cause this?*

I carefully tiptoe back to my bedroom. For now, I will keep the secret to myself.

~~~~~~~~~~~~~~~~~~~~~~~~

I remain in my room throughout the morning. Mother believes this is best since it is not safe to be outside. There is verification that Turkish and Kurd forces are approaching the village. My father slips out of our home, cautious to not be detected by the increasing number of patrols in the streets. I suspect his business has to do with the defense of Amasia.

I can no longer tolerate hiding the information from my parents about the foiled attempt on the sergeant's life. Mother listens to my involvement in what led to the death of Zaven. I am surprised by her calm demeanor as I blurt out the sordid details. Tears stream down my cheeks when my admission finally ends. Rather than scold me, she takes my hand and provides comfort.

"Your father and I surmised you were with your friends. It was foolish of you to participate in such a dangerous act. You were saved by the grace of God, but others died." I thought she misspoke, but the look in her eyes tells me something different. "Yes, your other friend has also died at the hands of the Turks." She uses her handkerchief to wipe my tears. Aram is gone because of our foolishness.

"Will they come for me, Mother?" I choke on the words, fearing her answer.

"We think not. The Turks have more important matters to deal with. There is great unrest in anticipation of a conflict." She refrains from calling it a battle, but I know exactly what she means.

My emotions are frazzled the rest of the day. Relief comes from having confided in my mother, but there is great sadness that two friends are gone. I continue to worry that the enemy will identify the third accomplice. If that happens, my entire family will suffer the consequences regardless of whether I used a weapon. Regretfully, this lesson in life comes with a high price. Darkness arrives, and I cry myself to sleep.

~~~~~~~~~~~~~~~~~~~~~~~~~~~~

I awaken before dawn to a sound in my bedroom. The room is filled with darkness, but there is no mistaking the shadowed figure seated beside my bed. Father has often entered my room upon arriving home from 'business' which I have now come to realize means fighting for a cause. He usually sits with a look of admiration and rarely speaks, but I always feel his gentle kiss before he retires to bed. However, tonight is different.

"Hello, Father. Is anything wrong?"

"No, son, everything is fine. You are safe and loved."

My father is a kind and gentle person. It is difficult to imagine him as a battle-hardened soldier. My eyes adjust to the darkness of the room and reveal that the man beside my bed is a warrior. The holstered sidearm at his waist and a Mauser rifle leaning against the chair give me cause to worry.

"Are you leaving, Father?"

"Yes, I must go now. Your mother and uncles will be with you." The assurance does little to alleviate my fear that something is terribly wrong.

"I'm afraid the bad people will come and hurt us. Please stay with me."

The response to my plea is a loving embrace. Then, he places a small cross into the palm of my hand. "The Lord will protect you when I am not here. Go back to sleep, my prince; morning will come soon."

"Father, once again you call me your prince. Will you tell me the meaning now?"

Yesterday's tragic event and the unrest coursing through our village weigh on the man that I admire most on this earth. He takes time to carefully consider an appropriate response. When he speaks, the words come softly from a humble man.

"It is true that we are simple people; we rule over no one. Our country has been invaded and conquered by other nations for centuries and yet, our legacy is to live on as Christians." It pains me to see tears in my father's eyes as he continues to

42

share something which I must never forget. "For now, my son, you need only to know that it is an endearing term that has special meaning." He says no more.

I wrap my arms around the man who has sacrificed everything for his family. He needs to know that I understand as I cherish this special moment between us.

The time comes when this man walks to the door to leave. At that moment, I do not see a warrior, just my father who loves me deeply.

Note: In 1894, Kurdish and Turkish troops carry out one the first great massacres of the Ottoman Empire when they pillage Sassoun. Thousands of Armenian men, women, and children are slaughtered. Folk hero, David of Sassoun, becomes a symbol of defiance and bravery astride his charging horse and brandishing his lightning sword. (Armenian Massacres and Turkish Tyranny)

Chapter 9

One day after the battle for Amasia a news correspondent arrives in Amasia ahead of the Turkish troops. He makes a quick stop at our home. I recognize him as someone who visited our home once before for an interview with my father. Mother asks Arixie and my uncles to join us in the kitchen as we listen to the man's story. He tells us that he is covering developments within the Ottoman Empire for an international news service and traveled with the Turkish troops when they approached our village.

"The Armenians didn't have much of a chance," he says, respectfully lowering his head, "They were outnumbered and pitted against a more superior force. I am one of the few correspondents to witness it. The Turks are very sensitive about what is reported by news agencies."

"I trust you will file an accurate report about what has happened to Amasia," Mother tells the man. His look is not encouraging.

"Mrs. Nighosian, I can write the report, but by the time the Otans alter it there will be no semblance to what I wrote.

"How is it that the rest of the world can ignore what is happening to our people?" Arixie asks. I see the anger in her face as she confronts the correspondent.

He appears sympathetic and attempts an explanation. "I understand your disappointment, but Armenia is only one of the travesties committed by powers of the Ottoman Empire. The Greeks, and other nationalities are facing similar situations."

The man adds a bit of information as a token of encouragement. "I recently learned that government officials in America are showing more attention to Armenia. Their ambassador, Henry Morgenthau, is rumored to be negotiating with the Ottomans regarding treatment of the Armenians. That might help the situation because the last thing the Turks want is to have the United States enter the war on the side of the Allies."

He becomes increasingly nervous. I think he fears the Turks may learn of his visit to our home. He quickly brings the meeting to an end. "The soldiers will be arriving soon. I must leave now. Please do not tell them about my visit. It could cost me my head."

~~~~~~~~~~~~~~~~~~~~~~~~~

"They were slaughtered!" Arixie shouts after the correspondent has left. "They had neither the weapons nor troops to fight against such an army." She informs us that she was busy early this morning gathering information about the brave men who challenged the invaders.

Mother makes the decision to allow me to listen. She takes my hand for support before asking something no one else is willing to venture. "And, the fate of my husband?"

Arixie searches for a kind response while my mother rests herself into a chair. The hurt already shows in her eyes.

"All of them... are gone," Arixie tells us.

~~~~~~~~~~~~~~~~~~~~~~~~~~~

The next day is hectic as talk spreads that enemy troops are preparing to capture the village. The perimeter is already secured by soldiers to prevent anyone from entering or leaving. No one is allowed outside their homes after dark. Our only hope is that friendly troops will arrive to rescue the citizens of Amasia. We are closer to neighboring Russia than the capital of Turkey near the Mediterranean Sea. The perception is that the Armenians living in the eastern section of the Ottoman Empire are more closely aligned with the neighboring non-Muslin nation. Officials in Constantinople know that the Russian army has crossed the border and is headed in our direction, but our time has run out.

~~~~~~~~~~~~~~~~~~~~~~~~~~~

It is the second day following the battle, and we grieve over the loss of my father. Arixie arrives in a panic. She informs us that her brothers are at risk of being taken by the Turks. Abraham and Yesa are of an age that draws the attention of our persecutors.

Their names are added to the dreaded list of those who are to be purged. The Turks use the awkward term to emphasize their disdain for the Christian Armenians.

"They'll either be taken to factories that manufacture munitions for the war or put to death. They must escape tonight. There will never be another opportunity," Arixie says.

"It's not safe to be on the streets, especially at night. How do you propose they get away without being seen?" Mother's question brings an immediate response.

"The rooftops," Arixie answers and glances toward our ceiling. "No one ever walks around looking at rooftops, especially a Turk. His big nose is always pointed to the ground." I am amused by the exaggeration, but the levity is brief. I eagerly listen to Arixie's explanation. "Your place is one of the few in Amasia that has access to the roof from inside the house."

I think to myself that she makes a good point. Not many years ago, my father constructed a closet stairway to have a rooftop flower garden. Mother delights in tending to her flowers without having to go out the front door. I doubt if anyone other than our family and Arixie are even aware of the hidden stairway. I now realize it has served a dual purpose in allowing my father to leave and return without being detected by enemy patrolling at night.

"If they escape the village, the challenge will be to board a ship on the Mediterranean Sea." Arixie's plan is not endorsed by everyone in the room.

"Much too dangerous," Mother interjects. "Constantinople and now the other port cities are swarming with Turks. Your brothers would be better to go northeast toward the Russian border. It is rough terrain, but the Russians are sympathetic to our cause, even if it is for the wrong reasons." I understand my mother's point. The Russians don't care about helping us for the noble cause of defending an oppressed Christian nation. They are more interested in our land and commerce.

"That makes sense. I will share it with my brothers." Now satisfied that her brothers have a chance to free themselves from Turkish tyranny, Arixie turns her cup to make a prediction. She's inspired by what the coffee drippings reveal. "Hmm, I see my brothers becoming prominent businessmen in another country. They share their good fortune with other people," she says with a proud smile. "Both are highly respected men who donate much to their community and church." I am fascinated by the creative storytelling and hope she will continue, but Mother discourages the notion. She knows our pleasant neighbor is prone to exaggerate. Right now, we have no assurance that Abraham and Yesa will even get out of the village alive.

It is a desperate attempt, but after midnight, Arixie's brothers enter the secret passageway. They cautiously make their way onto our roof. Abraham and Yesa wrap sheep's wool around their feet to muffle sounds as they leap from one roof to another. There are periods of long pauses while they remain hidden as patrols pass below them. I lie in bed imagining how frightened they must be to know that discovery means certain death. Everything is quiet for the longest time. Then, alarming sounds shatter the stillness of the night. Loud shouting comes from somewhere down the street. Several rifle shots cause me to fear the worse. The sounds coming through my open window fade into the distance, and silence returns to the streets.

I am awakened the next morning by loud cheering coming from the kitchen. Our daily guest arrives early to share something. I jump from my bed and rush to get the news. The scene is somewhat chaotic as our friend attempts to balance her two little ones on her lap between sips of coffee. She cannot contain her excitement.

"A-men eench lav e!" Arixie's voice is filled with excitement as she yells that everything is fine; the brothers made their escape. Mother offers a prayer of thanks. She takes my hand and the three

of us share the moment. We are grateful, and I remember someone special: *Father, thank you for the
secret stairway that saved the brothers. Your sacrifice for all of us will not be forgotten.*

Note: During World War I, both the Ottoman Empire and
Russia wanted to use the Armenians against their enemies.
The Armenians were caught in the middle of a world strug-
gle that found them used as pawns for either side. (Suny: A
History of the Armenian Genocide)

Chapter 10

One day passes, then another. I begin to think the Turkish Army may have called off the invasion, but it is just wishful thinking by a frightened youth. We continue to grieve over the loss of my father and the other brave protectors of Amasia. Mother worries that we are no longer safe in our home, so she requests my uncles stay with us.

On the third day, I accompany her to the open market located in the center of our village. Ara and Varge maintain watch over the house while we are gone. During the shopping trip, there will be an opportunity for me to visit with a much older friend. Mr. Yeghesian is my *gengahar,* a godfather and well-to-do merchant. He is a respected member of our community who is relied upon for financial support and advice. I am told that the personal 'loans' he makes to less fortunate people are not required to be repaid. This generous man is long into his senior years, yet he relates well with people of all ages. I like his perpetual smile, especially when he flashes four gold teeth, two in the front and two more in the back of his mouth. I'm looking forward to visiting a store that bears a sign, *Yeggi's Shop of Fine Tapestries.*

The military presence is not the only change I observe in our village. There are scattered families vacating their homes. People who have spent their entire lives in the same dwelling are loading belongings onto animals and carts. There are other obvious signs that the Turks have been busy during the days we were secluded in our home. Many Armenian shops are either closed or display signs announcing new ownership. One merchant selling his produce at the open market draws our attention. He is not one of the locals and his merchandise looks suspicious.

"Sir, I am interested in your fruits and vegetables," Mother says while examining a batch of okra. She sniffs the green vegetables for freshness and then looks over his array of fruits and vegetables. "Hmm, I see you also have fruit. I wonder if these apricots are fresh?" The man hesitates, but then he renders a safe answer.

"Why, yes, I believe you will find them to have excellent flavor." He offers one of the yellowish-orange fruits to sample. Mother wipes the apricot against her dress to remove any foreign particles and takes a small bite. She pauses to savor the flavor. Usually she zips from one merchant's booth to another, but today she takes her time. I have no clue why she delays making the purchase. On other occasions, I am invited to participate in the tasting. Today is different.

"May I taste the fruit, too?" Mother shakes her head to indicate I will remain an observer. I find this confusing, but she has her reasons.

"Madam are you pleased with the merchandise?" Instead of an answer, the vendor is asked to field another question.

"Are you aware of the theory that apricots actually originated in Armenia?" Mother asks. "I believe the site is near Garni."

"Uh, why no, I had not heard of that," the bewildered merchant responds. She is perplexed by the man's lack of knowledge associated with his trade, but he quickly returns to the business that can bring him money.

"It's just fruit, madam. Do you wish to buy it or not?" The fellow is impatient and has no interest in making small talk with a woman and her son. Mother wishes to stretch the conversation, so she gives him a satisfied response.

"The flavor is wonderful," she replies and continues to look over the quantity of fruit displayed before her. I have been ignored up to this point, but now the man smiles at me. I think he believes the cordial gesture will help make the sell, but his joy is premature. He still must contend with a woman who knows something isn't right.

"Do you think these apricots would be good for *A mar al din*?" Mother asks.

What follows is a long pause as the man posing as an honest merchant nervously shuffles his feet. I grow anxious with every passing moment of silence, especially when he cocks his chin and gives a defiant stare. He obviously doesn't have a clue related to the question but figures that any response may help to establish some credibility. He finally replies, "Well, probably not. It would make the stew too sweet."

My mother struggles to contain her composure as the man exposes his ignorance and confirms he knows little about apricots. He realizes it was a trap when she explains the reference was not about a pot of stew, but rather a drink made from apricots by ancient Egyptians. He mumbles a feeble excuse about having loss of memory, but the damage is already done. This supposed merchant has stirred a woman's scorn.

"I am certain you did not grow this produce yourself. Where did you get it?"

"What business is it of yours whether I grew it myself or bought it from someone? You can either buy it or move on!" He curses under his breath and waves a nasty gesture to signal he is finished with us.

"It *is* my business when someone steals from our family." Mother points to the baskets of produce and fires an accusation loud enough to be heard by other shoppers. "I believe this is the same produce our family harvested just days earlier. And, it was stolen!"

The man is irate. I step back and look for something to use as a weapon in case he becomes violent. The rocks along the street would be a foolish weapon against someone at least three times my size. The vendor knows he has the upper hand and uses it to his advantage.

"Woman, enough of your stupid interrogation! I paid a fair price for all of what you see, and that is what I will tell the soldiers. You and the boy should leave, or I will have you arrested."

The soldiers most likely receive favors for protecting this person's illicit operation. They will surely create any excuse to imprison us. We cannot win this encounter. Mother takes my hand and leads me away.

~~~~~~~~~~~~~~~~~~~~~~~~~~~~~~

Our final stop at the market is at Mr. Yeghesian's popular business. I am excited because I know there will be an ample supply of *lokoom* available to all visitors. The jellied candy contains pieces of walnuts and is coated in powdered sugar. Our friend, Yeggi, is kind and generous.

We encounter an expansive cluster of merchandise as soon as we enter the establishment. I stop to sample the free jellied treats while admiring the piles of tapestry we must maneuver around to reach the rear of the sales room. There are carpets on the floor, stacked on tables, displayed on racks, and even carpets hooked from the ceiling. They all share a common theme; each one of them features decorative designs in striking hues of color. I am fascinated by the beauty of the workmanship and the way stories are depicted in the threads. The many pieces surrounding me are the work of true artisans who have captured history in the ornate tapestries. Every stitch is hand-woven, a talent passed from one generation of Armenians to the next. Some of the carpets have the name of the family or person who created it woven into the fabric. One must carefully study the design to discover this unique feature.

We go to the back of the shop and approach a large man seated behind the rustic wooden counter. Smoke from a cigar clenched between his teeth encircles the red turban askew on his head as he reads a newspaper. His feet are propped on a pile of small carpets. It seems strange that Mr. Yeghesian would allow an employee to put his dirty boots on such nice weavings. The reason becomes obvious when Mother asks about the proprietor.

"Where is Yeggi, the owner?" she asks. Her familiarity tips the man off that the owner is a friend.

"I don't know anyone named Yeggi," he replies without lifting his eyes off the newspaper. "If you mean the old man that was here before me, well, he retired." He pauses to flick away ashes that have fallen onto a vest missing all but the center button. The worn piece of material is stretched to the limit and fails to contain a massive belly. I find some humor in this picture imagining that at any moment the stitching will burst and fire the final button from a three-hundred pound human cannon. Mother is focused on more serious matters.

"Retired? I don't believe it. I was in this shop just three days ago. Yeggi said nothing regarding retirement." She seldom raises her voice, but today is an exception. The tone is sharp and accusatory. "Sir, you are mistaken!" The man puts aside the newspaper and folds his arms across his chest. He takes exception to the insinuation he is lying. "Madam, I suggest you and the boy leave my establishment or I shall report you." "Really? You would have me arrested for inquiring why you are pretending to own this establishment. I know that you cannot possibly be the proprietor." He ignores the accusation and blows a puff of smoke in our direction. Mother pursues the inquisition. "Well, are you going to give me an answer or just sit there staring like a *gabeeg*?" The loathsome man is unfazed by the inference that he is a monkey.

"I will do my talking to the gendarmes when they arrive."

I worry about this threat. The gendarmes recently arrived in our village under the pretense of keeping order as a civilian police force. Our peaceful community never needed such a unit in prior years. Now, every adverse encounter with a Turk or Kurd ends with another Armenian citizen being taken away and never seen again. I think the gendarmes are only here to safeguard the interests of an increasing number of foreign merchants infiltrating Amasia and other communities.

"Mother, I think we should leave." She resists the tug of my hand.

"Not yet, Nishan. Not until I find out what has happened to Mr. Yeghesian."

The obese merchant decides to confront his accuser and leans forward attempting to get up. He struggles and reverts to shifting his weight back and forth in a chair that is not made for rocking. I wonder if we should try to help, but Mother indicates the man has already suffered enough embarrassment. He seems to have followed this routine on other occasions. Eventually, one of the forward motions thrusts his body into a standing position. The glowing cigar remains propped in his mouth, although a new batch of ash has fallen onto the vest. He delivers a nasty ultimatum.

"Lady, if you don't leave my shop right now, I'm sure the gendarmes will have their pleasure with you and the boy." The message is clear as he taunts me by rubbing his hands together. Graphic stories already circulate telling of perverted acts upon Armenian women and young persons by the invading army and its civilian police force. We have no alternative but to leave. For now, Mother has lost the argument but perhaps saved my life.

The trip to the market brings the realization that our society, culture and heritage are being sacrificed. One day, Mr. Yeghesian is part of our lives, and then he is gone.

Note: Frances Willard, leader of the Women's Christian Temperance Union, roused England and America to help the Armenians during the early genocide. She raised money for the migration of Armenians to England and the U.S. She spoke out against the massacre of Armenians by the Turks. (Wikipedia: Frances Willard and the Armenian Crisis)

Chapter 11

Large contingents of soldiers arrive in the village two days later. Shouts throughout the streets announce their presence.

"Lock your doors! Stay inside!" The warnings are sometimes followed by gunfire as those sounding the alarm are permanently silenced. Mother rushes to make sure the front door is bolted. She instructs Ara and Varge to check the locks on the windows. We listen in silence for any indication of what may be happening outside. I am huddled on the floor in her arms; tears running down my cheeks soak the front of her blouse. The Turks have arrived in force and we are at their mercy.

Terrible sounds come from the streets for the next hour. They are faint at first and grow increasingly louder as soldiers make their way in the direction of our home. There is a systemic routine being followed. First comes the loud slam of a rifle butt against wooden doors. If the command of "Open up!" is ignored, there are a series of rupturing blows. Door hinges eventually falter and allow a rifle muzzle to fire into the dwelling. Those who decline to follow the initial order sacrifice much more than their belongings. The soldiers stop in front of Arixie's house and shout orders to open the door. They will be on our steps next. Mother whispers a prayer, "Lord, please be with her and the little ones."

We sit in silence, anticipating the sound of splintering wood coming from the house next door. I fear for Arixie and her children, but soon there is a strangely familiar voice yelling at the soldiers. Mother unbolts the front door and we look out.

Arixie begrudgingly has followed the order. She is now standing in her doorway defying the armed intruders. One hand rests on her hip while the other vigorously waves a large soup spoon in the air.

"Shame on you!" she shouts indignantly. "Each of you should be home caring for your families instead of waging war against women and children!" She continues to shake the wooden spoon while scolding them. Some of the befuddled soldiers have their heads lowered suggesting they agree with the angry lady, although they dare not reveal it to their superiors. Any soldier showing outward signs of empathy for the Armenians will endure harsh military discipline. No one intervenes on Arixie's behalf.

"No, no, don't antagonize them," Mother whispers to herself. We continue to watch the action taking place only a short distance from our home. I worry this may be the last time we see our neighbor alive, but I am mistaken. The ranking officer appears to be amused by a woman keeping his men at bay with nothing more than a utensil used for stirring soup. He determines our feisty neighbor poses no real threat and issues a warning that she faces severe punishment by continuing to be belligerent. The soldiers are ordered to move on.

The enemy now approaches our house.

~~~~~~~~~~~~~~~~~~~~~~~~~~~~

"Do not be afraid, Nishan," Mother tells me when the soldiers bang on our door. I want to be brave, but the fear is obvious when I bite my lip trying to hold back tears. She opens the door and asks in a calm voice, "What is it you want?"

"All Armenians are to immediately evacuate the village," the officer commands. "You have ten minutes to gather any belongings to carry with you."

"Why are you doing this?" Mother asks without raising her voice. The officer appears exasperated by the same question he has repeatedly been asked throughout the morning. He idly gazes down the street and responds in a monotone.

"The Russian Army is approaching this sector of Armenia. You are being deported to a new location." He looks her squarely in the eyes and lies. "It is for your own safety."

"And, if we do not wish to leave?" She is not easily intimidated, but the officer is clearly fed up. He terminates the conversation in cruel fashion.

"Then you and the rest of your family will suffer the same fate as your husband, Mrs.

Neghosian." His hand grasps the hilt of a saber to emphasize the gravity of the threat.

Mother's eyes glisten as she contemplates the possible repercussions of her reply. Thoughts of my father's sacrifice must weigh heavily on the decision. I know her thoughts are for the safety of others when she softly responds, "We will comply with your request and gather our things."

The next minutes are frantic as we hurriedly prepare for the forced evacuation. Mother shouts assignments as she works in the kitchen packing food into containers. She makes sure to include a large supply of spices and other ingredients. We will not have the animals to carry any of it since they must be left behind. Supposedly, they are to be used in the war effort, but more likely to become the personal booty of our captors.

"Varge, get the water jugs we use for trips to the farm. Fill them to the top and make sure you tighten the caps." She wraps a generous slab of basturma in cheesecloth and continues calling out instructions. "Ara, strip the sheets off the beds. If we make it through the mountain passages, the desert sun will bake us. Gather some clothes when you finish." My uncles rush to different parts of the house. I am anxious to hear what is assigned to me. "Nishan, go to your room and fill a pillowcase with clothes, nothing heavy." I follow her instructions and only pause to consider what articles of clothing are clean and which are dirty. It is a silly notion;

cleanliness is not a priority under these circumstances.

Time is running out when I return to the kitchen. Ara places a bundle of sheets next to the front door and starts down the steps to assist Varge with the water jugs. Mother calls for him to bring up a large bundle of grape leaves that are stored in the coolness of the cellar room. She hurries back to the kitchen to arrange containers of food into two satchels. I once believed my father used the encasements for important documents during his travels to Constantinople. I now think the leather pouches probably transported ammunition to the freedom fighters.

The soldiers are back, and Mother has one final task for me before we leave the house. "Nishan, go to my room. Bring the small book on the table next to the bed." There is pounding on the front door. The soldiers will break in if we do not respond in a matter of seconds. I rush to the rear bedroom and look for the item that Mother refuses to leave behind. "Hurry, Nishan, we must leave now!"

I snatch the book she reads each night and return to her side just as the latch on the front door creaks open. Mother grabs the item from me and wraps it with a hand towel. She slips the small bundle of cloth into the pocket of her dress. For now, the Holy Bible is safely hidden from the non-Christian invaders.

We exit the house and see chaos in the streets. Hundreds of bewildered people are displaced from their homes in a matter of minutes. The gendarmes are herding them into lines as though they are animals going to slaughter. It is useless to resist because the police force is reinforced by soldiers of the invading army. The uniforms may be different, but their mission is the same- deport and eradicate the Armenians.

Arixie's young family joins us in the street. She cuddles the baby-daughter in one arm while the crying toddler clutches her skirt. A large bag with food and clothing is on the ground next to her. She cannot possibly care for the children and carry the cumbersome bundle, so my uncle Varge hoists it onto his shoulder.

One man in uniform stands out as he shouts orders. Sgt. Asid, while not fully recovered from his earlier wounds, continues to torment the besieged citizens. "Move them out," he orders and waves his saber toward the mountain pass south of Amasia. "Escort anyone that refuses to leave to the church."

For a moment there appears to be an alternative to exiting our village. Mother looks up and down the crowded street and a worried look comes over her. Something is not right. The soldiers are forcing several men into a separate group. "Where are they taking all of the old men?" she asks. Then she cries out to everyone around us. "They are seizing the elders of our village!"

"Sgt. Asid ordered them to assemble outside the church. He told them they will be transported to factories for work during the war," Arixie informs us. "Those men are too old to work in a factory making ammunition." Mother shakes her head to negate the story. "There is more to this than he's telling us."

Many wives refuse to leave the men, so soldiers use bayonets fixed on rifle barrels to prod them in the direction of the church. Sgt. Asid has no compassion for the people that have spent a lifetime together. "Keep them separated," he barks a command. "Lock the women inside the church! Leave the men outside near the east wall!" The slow procession heads toward the church located near the center of the village. Mother becomes suspicious when a crippled man missing an arm struggles to carry his duffle bag. A soldier pushes him forward and shouts, "Leave it here; you won't need it when the vultures claim your bones."

We stand in line for several minutes while the soldiers search people for weapons and other items. Money and valuables are confiscated; those who resist feel the butt of a rifle or worse. Our people eventually begin their movement through the streets leading out of town. The soldiers do not hesitate to use whips, bayonets, and swords on anyone who lags; steel blades save bullets. Mother reminds our small group to remain close together.

I see something that makes me sick to my stomach when we turn a corner. Two people hang from make-shift gallows. Their heads droop, but I recognize the man and woman. Zaven's aunt and uncle have also paid the ultimate price for the

66

botched attack on the sergeant. I stare at the lifeless bodies of people who often welcomed me into their home. Sgt. Asid has purposely chosen this route, so the entire village will see these good people hanging on public display. The nausea becomes worse when a soldier warns me, "See what happens when boys try to act like men? The whole family dies!" He accentuates the threat by making a throat-cutting gesture and proceeds with a taunting laugh that echoes down the street.

Mother thinks better than to elevate the situation, but Arixie shows no hesitation. She hands Ara her daughter and confronts the vile soldier. "Leave the boy alone, you Turkish dog!" The soldier draws back the butt of his rifle preparing to strike a blow, but another soldier intervenes.

"Don't waste your energy on her. The journey to Aleppo or Deir ez Zor will take care of her soon enough." I have heard of the places he mentions. They are in the desert hundreds of miles from our village. We will die before reaching our destination. The offending soldier backs away, but not before he sends a wad of spit in Arixie's direction. Both uncles step forward to confront the man.

"Don't be foolish!" Mother intervenes. "He's only trying to incite you to have an excuse to put you on the gallows. Now, both of you calm down and get back in line." She conveys another message as the two distance themselves from the offending soldier. "There will be other opportunities for revenge. First, we must survive a mountain and the desert."

We come to the holy place of worship. The Greek Orthodox Church with its ornate dome represents the symbol of our belief in the Christian faith. It is usually a peaceful location, but not today. There are screams emitting through the walls of the sacred building. Many Armenian women are locked behind heavy wooden doors. I cover my ears to block the sounds of torture. The old men are being guarded on one side of the church.

"Mother, where are the trucks to transport the men to the factories?" She hears me, but an answer will not be forthcoming.

"Keep walking and do not look back." She tightens her grip on my hand and hurries our pace.

It is only when our long line of humanity is beyond the village borders that sounds of execution gunfire erupt from somewhere behind us. A volley tell us the elders of our village have been executed. Soon after, a large plume of smoke blackens the sky. The church is ablaze with the women locked inside.

Our journey in the face of death has begun.

Note: By 1915, the Turkish Army suffered defeat in most battles against the Russian Army in the Caucasus Mountains of Armenia. In addition, the Turks lost nearly 100,000 men due to typhus and dysentery caused by inadequate medical and sanitary services. (AGBU: Ambassador Morgenthau's Story)

Chapter 12

We are now deportees from Amasia. They categorize Armenians in this manner because by mid-afternoon, others have joined the caravan from villages in the region. I do not recognize the people, although we share something in common. We are all persecuted because of our nationality and faith.

There is little conversation as the Turk and Kurd guards continue to threaten us with whips and bayonets. Every now and then someone unfamiliar to me nods to my mother. I come to realize that it confirms my father's reputation among our people has spread beyond Amasia. This simple gesture brings forth memories of the man who called me his prince: *Father, you were such a kind man who wanted nothing more than to raise your family in a peaceful nation. I am sorry you died trying to fulfill the dream.*

The pace is slow. Our people are accustomed to rigorous daily labor; however, the journey through mountain passes is arduous and dangerous. The forced march takes its toll. When people faulter, others rush to their aid for fear the soldiers will put a lethal end to the suffering.

"This is not good," Arixie whispers, as she shuffles along. We'll all be dead before we ever reach the desert."

"Hush up," Mother says, not wishing to alarm people who already have lost so much. "We will get through the mountain and we *will* survive." She pauses to make an affirmation loud enough to be heard by the soldiers keeping us in the line. "My husband and our men did not give their lives for us to simply perish on a mountain or in the desert at the hands of infidels. They died for us to live! Now, walk with your heads held high my friends and neighbors, for we are the faithful Armenians and the Lord is our savior!"

Cheering erupts along the human chain. This is our first demonstration of enthusiasm since being deported. It is quelled only when soldiers on horseback use their long whips on the demonstrators. An officer gives Mother a stern admonishment.

"Mary Nighosian! Any more trouble out of you will result in swift punishment, and not just for you!" He points to our huddled group and singles out each one- first, Arixie and the children, then Varge, then Ara, and finally me. My family and friends are marked people for the rest of the journey.

By late afternoon, most people have exhausted the small supply of liquid they were able to carry. They now rely on a meager ration of water provided by our captors. Two soldiers assigned to a tank truck distribute four ounces of water to each person during rest stops.

"No one can exist on less than a quart of water while walking all day," Arixie says to the corporal charged with distributing the water. "You are trying to annihilate the entire nation of Armenia."

The soldier is not moved by her indignation. His response is cruel. "You may be right, lady, and we will do it without wasting any ammunition." He takes the ladle filled with Arixie's ration of water and pitches it into the air. "So, I guess you won't be needing this."

We travel eleven miles from our village by nightfall. The physical and mental strain leaves little energy for making camp. The mountain air is chilling, but we are not allowed to have a campfire. Mother reminds us that the trek will be long, so we must conserve energy and supplies whenever possible. She packed an ample quantity of food but only hands out small portions of basturma and choreg. No one objects to the meager amount because we know there are many others suffering in the camp. Scattered among the foliage are a few plants containing berries and even some grape leaves like the bundle that came from our food cellar. She intends to add them to the food supply if they can be harvested before the soldiers get them. Fortunately, the guards prefer to rest. I sense my mother is formulating a plan and prefers to keep it a secret for the time being. Varge and Ara spread blankets on the ground for each of us. The sheep's wool is a barrier from the cold earth of the mountain.

If there is any relief from the sadness on this night, it comes from the voice of someone approaching. "Hello friends! May I come into your camp?" I am shocked to see Mr. Yeghesian emerge from the darkness. Mother rushes to the friend we thought had perished.

"Yeggie! Yeggi! Yes, please join us!" She gives him an affectionate hug and lightly kisses his cheek. It is a joyful reunion, although my godfather no longer displays his usual wide smile. Uncle Varge tells me it is likely because of the hardship we have all encountered, but I believe there is something different about Yeggi that he prefers not to divulge. The others eventually return to setting up the campsite, but I remain with the newest member of our party.

"Nishan, it is so good to see you." He wraps his arms around me and raises me off the ground. It is surprising that a man of his age who trekked many miles with little food or water can be so vigorous, but Mr. Yeghesian is no ordinary person. In fact, he is tall and slender which is rather unusual since most Armenians generally reach only medium height. Yes, he is old, but his frame remains strong and erect. I am filled with curiosity, so I try to pose the question.

"I thought... I thought you were... uh, uh," The fatal word fails me, but Yeggi squints an eye letting me know he's already figured it out.

"Hmm, I believe we have a quandary here," he says while scratching the stubble of beard on his chin. "Let me rest these weary bones and I will be happy to answer your question." He takes a seat on the ground and removes his shoes. "Ahh, that feels better. Come join me, Nishan, and hear how I managed to stay alive." He pats the ground next to him and I accept the invitation. "Now, I believe you were asking about my near-death." The old sage has a unique command of language, even when speaking about his own demise. He notices my sheepish look for having raised the question. "You needn't be embarrassed. You're not the first person to believe that I joined the angels in heaven." He smiles but avoids flashing those beautiful gold teeth.

"Thank you, sir. I would really like to know how you managed to stay alive."

"Actually, I thought it was all over for me when two soldiers escorted me out of my shop. They locked me in a shed. Heaven only knows why they didn't just put me against a wall and shoot me." He muses about his good fortune before continuing. "I now realize they were just keeping me alive until the evacuation. I had to do something; otherwise, I would be one of those unfortunate souls executed at the church."

"So, how did you get away?"

"Well, something I've learned during my lifetime is that the Turks love to barter, so I traded with them." There's a twinkle in his eyes indicating a surprise is coming.

"What could you possibly have to barter? Didn't they take all your valuables when they raided your shop?"

"Not quite everything." Yeggi takes a moment to scan the area to make sure no one is eavesdropping. Satisfied that we are alone, he breaks into a big smile. My jaw drops open when I see a gaping hole that once held two gold front teeth.

"Yeggi, your shiny teeth are gone!" My elderly friend shows no alarm and calmly continues his story.

"You need not feel sorry for me, Nishan. I have a secret to tell you." His eyes once again shift back and forth checking to see we are still alone. The suspense makes me nervous. He leans closer and whispers into my ear, "I think it was a good deal-two gold teeth for one life." Yeggi slaps his knee in laughter, quite satisfied with himself for maintaining the interest of an impressionable youth. The joyfulness exposes his entire mouth and I notice something strange. Where are the other gold teeth?

"Oh, yes. You're wondering about the other ones? Well, my inquisitive friend, allow me to show you how I outsmarted the scoundrels." He uses his forefinger to pick around the spot where the gold teeth once set. I impatiently wait as more fingers are used to manipulate inside his mouth. Then, a sharp yank of the hand causes his head to jerk backward. I am startled as three fingers emerge clutching a huge wad of juiced tobacco. He runs his tongue along the back of the mouth and spits the brown-stained saliva onto the ground. The continued cleansing reveals what was hidden under the tobacco. The 'missing' gold teeth are firmly intact.

We sit together for a few more minutes. The misery of today's journey is temporarily postponed. Yeggi and I gaze into a sky sprinkled with stars, just a pleasant, smiling elderly man and his young friend. My eyes glisten with admiration for this person who represents a nation of survivors.

Note: The Turkish government, taking advantage of the military actions of German forces issues a special order on April 24, 1915, to exterminate the Armenians of Western Armenia. The result is the slaughter of 1.5 million people and more than 600,000 are driven into the Mesopotamian deserts, where most of them perish.
(Rem Ananikyan: Yerevan)

Chapter 13

I visit with my mother after saying goodnight to the kindly rug merchant. Her attention is focused on our neighbor from Amasia. Arixie is weak from the journey but continues to care for her children. She helps the boy find pebbles to play with and then begins to nurse her infant daughter. Lately, the child has been crying more often.

"My body is drying up," Arixie says. "My 'sweet flower' cannot get enough milk for her tiny body."

"You need to start weaning her right away. She must learn to process goat's milk," Mother advises. "I know it is difficult to deprive her but giving her less now may help save her life." Arixie allows the baby to suckle only for a short time. Denying nourishment brings forth an episode of incessant crying. It would be quite annoying under normal circumstances, but the rigors of the day have taken a toll. No one complains; we are thankful the little one is still alive.

The camp is not well-organized during our first night of captivity. There are no toilet facilities for hundreds of refugees and little time to dig latrines. People take care of their bodily functions in the foliage or shed all modesty to eliminate waste in the open. Darkness provides a measure of privacy, so I slip into some bushes and drop my trousers. I am close enough to the water truck to overhear two soldiers seated next to a small fire. One is the corporal that Arixie confronted earlier. Neither man is pleased with the evening meal.

"Porridge! That is what those sons-of-bitches in Constantinople give us for food," the lowly private complains and spits out a mouthful of gray mash. "And all the while, they're dining on shish-kebab and wine that *we* raided from the Armenians!"

"You better keep your mouth shut, or we will both be joining the Armenians on the death march," the corporal warns.

"So, what? At least we'd have something more than grains mixed in boiling water to keep us alive," the private counters. The angry chatter continues, and I learn there is considerable dissention within the Turkish ranks. It is no longer safe to remain hidden. Someone may come looking for me and accidently expose me to the soldiers. I pull up my trousers and cautiously slip away.

Everyone is trying to get some well-deserved rest. Mother continues to watch for my safe return. I approach her with my head lowered. Leaving my body waste in the bushes is embarrassing. She smiles affectionately and tells me to lie next to her. I feel safe in her arms and share information about the disgruntled soldiers.

"That's interesting, Nishan. Perhaps it can be an advantage to us." She does not elaborate and shifts her thoughts to my well-being. "You should sleep now. Tomorrow will be a long day." She reaches into her dress pocket and retrieves the small book which has been safely hidden since we left the village. I drift to sleep as she quietly reads a passage from the Holy Bible, "Don't be afraid, for the Lord will go before you and will be with you; He will not fail nor forsake you."

My sleep is restless. The moans and cries of so many people cannot be blocked. They ache from the long march along the mountain trails, but the real pain comes from our loss of people and identity. Throughout the campsite are many who do not have the essentials to shield them from nature's elements. There are those with such limited food supplies that they opt to rest on empty bellies. The old people who avoided being put to death in the village are very weak. What little body muscle they retain has been used to the limit. I get little rest knowing that tomorrow will be worse than today.

~~~~~~~~~~~~~~~~~~~~~~~~~~~~~

Mother's evening is not ended. The conversation at the water truck intrigues her. She delays sleeping to pursue an idea triggered from my eavesdropping. After checking to make sure everyone in our group is resting peacefully, she leaves our camp and makes her way to where I described the soldiers are camped. Mother's movement alerts my troubled sleep and I refuse to let her go on this mission alone. I follow her from a distance to make sure she is safe.

The two men are still bickering at their camp-fire. They are startled by movement in the under-brush and grab their rifles. I remain hidden in the bushes as Mother approaches them.

"Who is there? Show yourself or be shot!"

"It is I, Mary Nighosian." She steps forward in-to the illuminating glow of the fire.

"What is it you want, woman?" the corporal shouts. "If it is food, we have none for you. Go back to your people!"

"I did not come for food. However, we are in dire need of it and other supplies."

The soldiers are devoid of compassion. They make their position perfectly clear. "That's enough talk, woman. Be gone or you will never have need of food again." The corporal cocks his rifle to back up the threat. Mother steps back fearing the man will pull the trigger, but she intends to fulfill her mission.

"Sir, I merely wish to offer my service to you." Her soft-spoken composure baffles the two men who are accustomed to people cowering before them.

The corporal is inquisitive. "What possible ser-vice can you offer soldiers of the Ottoman Empire? Armenians no longer have anything that we need."

Mother is not intimidated by the hollow boast-ing of a soldier who already expressed his anguish toward the regime he serves. She gives an enticing response. "A fine meal of tomato-stewed grape leaves filled with delicious meat and vegetables." She pauses to let the men contemplate her proposition. A reply comes forth in mere seconds.

"Come closer, Mary Nighosian. Sit by the fire and tell us more." Both men set aside their weapons and place another cushion on the ground.

The following minutes are filled with intriguing conversation. She engages the two soldiers with tales of wonderful meals prepared for dignitaries of the Ottoman Empire who visited with my father. The stories are not exaggerated too much because our current food supply is limited. By the time she finishes, the hungry soldiers are anxious to sample her talent for cooking.

The arrangement becomes more appetizing when she claims, "With the proper ingredients, I can make anything seem quite tasty, even porridge." It is an alliance froth with opportunity and danger for each party. The soldiers face strict discipline if they are discovered bartering favors from an Armenian. Our own people will surely be opposed to collaborating with the enemy, even if it is done with good intentions.

"What do you expect in return for your cooking services?" asks the skeptical corporal.

"I require a greater ration of water for our people. Four ounces a few times a day is not enough to sustain our bodies, especially if we reach the desert. We need at least twice that amount." The offer of tastier food may not be enough incentive, so she increases the stakes. "Besides, it will not bode well for either of you if your superiors find out so many of our people died of thirst due to your negligence."

The men discuss the proposition between themselves. They quarrel back and forth. The private is not afraid of what his superiors might do if the Armenians die. He rationalizes that the whole purpose of the march into the desert is to get rid of the Armenians. The corporal thinks more about his stomach than the consequences for an alliance with an Armenian. He doesn't favor bargaining with my mother, but the notion of tastier food has great appeal. He suggests a compromise. "Six ounces and that is all I can do." Mother hesitates to accept the offer, so the corporal explains his rationale. "Sgt. Asid will take a saber to our heads if he suspects we are aiding you. The amount you request will be too easy for him to detect." She believes the man speaks the truth and accepts the concession. Two more ounces of water during each break is not much, but it could mean the difference between life and death.

Both men extend their hands to seal the deal, but Mother declines to shake hands with men who wear the uniform of an army that murdered my father. She binds the agreement with a simple statement, "I am Armenian. You can trust me to keep *my* end of the bargain." The men understand the innuendo, but let it pass for now. She requests one more concession before ending the conversation. "We need a daily measure of goat's milk."

The corporal fidgets while considering the request. He is skeptical of giving up too much in the deal. After satisfying a persistent itch on his hind end, a reply indicates he's through negotiating. "There will be no free milk! You must pay for it and not with food."

"Sir, the soldiers have taken everything. We have no money or property. Please, I beg of you to grant this request.

"Beg all you want, Mrs. Nighosian. No money; no goat's milk. Now, go back to your camp or we have no agreement. It will do no good to plea any longer." The discussion ends.

~~~~~~~~~~~~~~~~~~~~

I rush back to our campsite and slip under the blanket pretending to be asleep when Mother returns. I imagine that she is joyful at having secured an arrangement of more water for the deportees, but the quest for milk to nourish Arixie's infant has failed. The deal struck with the two Turkish soldiers is a shallow victory.

Everyone at the camp is asleep except for Yeggi. He, too, must have observed my mother slipping out of camp. That means he also observed me. He motions for me to quietly join him and together we approach Mother. She gives a loving smile when she sees the two of us.

"Mary, we have waited for you," Yeggie says softly while keeping the three of us partially hidden in the shadows of night. I am relieved that my friend does not betray the fact that I followed Mother from the camp.

"Oh, Yeggi, I didn't expect anyone to still be awake."

"We were worried about you. Are you alright?"

"Yes, I'm fine. You needn't have worried. I was on an errand."

"You say an errand? That sounds rather strange under these circumstances." He makes a case for his skepticism. "We are many miles from our village and being held hostage in a wilderness by Ottoman soldiers. Yes, I believe going on an errand is rather peculiar."

"I'm sorry, Yeggi. I did not mean to deceive you. If I am to tell anyone, it might as well be the most trusted person in the land." She shares the arrangement made with the soldiers. I listen to her explanation and it is just as I overheard while hiding in the bushes at the Turkish campsite.

"I believe you bargained well, Mary, but you shouldn't expose yourself to such danger. The Turks cannot be trusted under any circumstances," he warns.

"Well, maybe not such a good deal," Mother replies, turning away to hide her tears.

"I don't understand, Mary. Tell me why you are so sad." Yeggi takes her hand and gives an assurance. "It's okay to tell me. After all, I'm much too old to remember the secrets people confide in me." The bit of humor is comforting.

"I failed to secure milk for the baby. Without it, she will die. The Turks want money, and we have none."

"Now I understand the dilemma." Our friend mulls over the predicament. He then gives a response that is shadowed in mystery. "I may have a solution to the problem, but it is somewhat complicated. You get some well-deserved sleep. Perhaps tomorrow will be a better day."

It will be a short night, but I finally fall asleep knowing that my mother is safe and wondering what the Armenian godfather has in store for us.

Note: Andranik Ozanian, Commander of the Armenian Revolutionary Forces, led numerous engagements against Ottoman troops, often winning battles in spite of being outnumbered. He later joined allied forces as a general in the Russian Army. He was a leader who inspired troops to victory. (Suny: A History of the Armenian Genocide)

Chapter 14

Morning comes too early as a shrill horn breaks through the crisp mountain air. The rising sun sends sparkles of light between the peaks. Under different circumstances, I would marvel at the majestic beauty of our land. Now it reminds me that we are hostages facing another day of forced march.

I rise from a blanket that served as my mattress during the night. It did little to separate me from the cold, hard dirt. Mother is nowhere to be seen, but soon I hear her voice as she emerges from the underbrush carrying a bundle of grape leaves. She must have picked the tender sprouts in the cover of darkness. I think only a person with her years spent in a kitchen could possibly harvest this foliage just by feeling its texture. Her cheerful greeting is void of any indication that we are in peril.

"Good morning, dear one. I hope you had a good sleep," she says and carefully spreads the grape leaves on a blanket.

"You should not have left in the dark. I was afraid for you."

She puts my fears to rest. "You needn't worry. My heart is always with you, even when you can't see me." She kisses my forehead to seal the promise.

There is little time for amenities. The soldiers are rushing people to form lines and evacuate the camp. Breakfast consists of a small portion of *katah*. In past times, this form of coffee cake served with sweetened milk was always a special treat. Its purpose today is to keep us alive. The milk is just a memory; it is now substituted by a scant amount of water.

People briefly exit our group to take care of bodily functions wherever it is convenient. Guards are suspicious of anyone who strays too far. It is better to sacrifice privacy rather than to risk losing one's life for fear of embarrassment. I help Uncle Ara collect the blankets and other items used during the night. Uncle Varge is busy taking care of Arixie's boy. She is having difficulty nursing the baby. The loud cries of an infant seem to be a plea for an entire nation.

"My body is nearly empty," Arixie whimpers as tears dampen her soiled dress. "My little 'sweet flower' is growing weaker. She needs more milk than I can produce." Silence is an indication that all of us share Arixie's suffering.

The soldiers are not sympathetic. They continue to harass anyone who appears to be stalling. A hideous scream comes every so often and another person succumbs to the Turkish blade. Mother closely watches as we assemble. Suddenly, she shouts, "I don't see Yeggi! He's gone!" Ara and Varge attempt to search for him, but soldiers threaten death to anyone who strays. We are about to give up hope of ever seeing our friend again, but then he appears and takes a place in the line next to me.

"Good morning, young man." Yeggi smiles and places a comforting hand on my shoulder. The cordial greeting is too casual. My inquisitive look brings a trite explanation. "Sorry to alarm everyone. I was just taking care of business." I believe there is more to the story, but there is no time to elaborate; the forced march begins on day two.

Our section of captives moves past the encampment. What is left behind is now revealed. The area is littered with belongings that seemed important a day ago. Now these items are nonessential. Heavy wool coats, cooking utensils, and framed pictures of family members are scattered throughout the grounds. However, the most telling evidence of Turkish control brings sorrow to my heart. The bodies of those who either perished trying to escape or from exposure are left to rot and be ravaged by wild animals.

The morning hours add more people from provinces. Now, thousands stretch for miles and are secured by increasing numbers of military vehicles and troops. It is blatantly obvious that the 'safe evacuation' of Armenian communities is a ploy to destroy an entire nation. One of the new arrivals works his way through the line to reach us.

"Are you the wife of Osigian Nighosian?" Mention of the name brings back heartfelt memories of the man who loved me. Mother tells me to slow down so we can walk with the elderly man.

"Yes, Osigian was my husband. He is no longer among the living." She studies the man's features but does not recognize him.

"I heard he died in the battle at Amasia. He was a great man." The stranger has Mother's attention.

She speaks softly to avoid being overheard by the guards. "Thank you for those kind words. Tell me how you know my husband?" Her eyes look straight ahead to avoid drawing attention to the conversation.

"I never personally met Osigian, but my grandson fought beside him in many engagements. He shared tales of your husband's bravery whenever he returned home. Nicholas was a good boy." There is sadness in the stranger's tone of voice.

"Where is your grandson now?" Mother asks.

"He is now with the Lord." The man shakes his head grieving, "Only nineteen... much too young."

"I am sorry for your loss," Mother says and grasps the man's hand. She looks into his eyes and gives a reassurance. "You will be in my prayers tonight. Be at peace, my friend, your Nicholas rests with the Lord."

The three of us continue walking in silence. Eventually, the man slows his pace and bids farewell. He fades into the mass of people behind us. We shall never see him again, but what I learned from my mother during this brief encounter will stay with me for a lifetime: *There are no strangers when it comes to kindness and compassion.*

The military trucks hauling troops and pulling cannons have difficulty traversing the ravines and steep rock formations of the mountain. The march is halted when vehicles become lodged by boulders or mired in mud. Our men are forced to labor trying to free equipment that the Turks consider more important than human life. We will reach a plateau region in one more day, so the present rough terrain affords the best opportunity to make an escape. Several attempts already have ended in death. Our captors prefer public executions. We are halted at locations close to steep cliffs and made to witness persons thrown over the edge. Listening to the hideous scream of someone hurtling a thousand feet to their death serves as a strong deterrent for others wanting to flee. The Turks resort to beheadings on occasions when the landscape does not provide for this cruel form of punishment.

"Do not look, Nishan," Mother says as we approach the result of an execution. I turn my head aside and stare at the ground.

"No, no, no!" a guard shouts and rushes toward me. He puts a dirty hand on my neck and forces me to view the results of a decapitation.

"Leave me alone!" I try to break free of his strong grip. He uses the other hand to knock me down. Then he presses my face into the dirt. I cannot breathe. Mother desperately tries to help me, but other soldiers restrain her.

"Whap!" A sharp blow to the head sends my attacker tumbling. I brush the dirt from my eyes and see Uncle Varge on top of the assailant. "Whap!" Varge lands another punch. The soldier is clearly overmatched and covers his head trying to fend off the blows. Three other soldiers attempt to aid their comrade, but Uncle Ara throws his body in front of them and they tumble to the ground. Now the count is two against four, and the uncles are winning the fight. Years of honing their muscles working the farm and orchard have made them more than a match for the loathsome soldiers. Mother rushes to my side when the man guarding her joins in the brawl. It's five against two. There is no help for the uncles as other guards threaten to execute anyone who dares to interfere. For the moment, it is a small victory for our people as two Armenian brothers strike blows against the Ottoman Empire. The soldiers are battered into submission and cheering erupts as the news is passed along the line. Ultimately, more uniformed men overwhelm the two and pin them to the ground.

"Lop their heads," one of the guard's shouts. The brothers are forced to their knees with their hands tied behind them. A soldier draws his saber and raises it high above his head. The razor-sharp blade reflects sunlight as the executioner prepares to strike the death blow. I am a helpless prisoner, but I refuse to witness the execution of two people who risked their lives for me. I close my eyes and await the swishing sound of the curved blade.

"Hold your sword!" A command rips the air and captures everyone's attention. I open my eyes and see a rider galloping toward our location. He tugs at the reins and brings his mount to an abrupt stop only a few feet from me. I dread looking at the mangled face of Sgt. Asid.

The man's squinting eyes assess the situation. "Put them in chains," he says pointing at the brothers. Then he gives a disgusting look at the five combatants on the ground and issues an admonishment. "You are an embarrassment to the Ottoman Empire. There will be even more punishment for you when we reach our destination."

A hateful expression sends wrinkles across the hideous scars on his face when he recognizes the two who are about to be executed. "Praise Allah! I know these Christian Armenians." He is not the only one making a connection. Mother acknowledges the notorious enemy of the Armenian people.

"Yes, and I know you are the butcher of women and children." Her disdain for the villainous sergeant supersedes concern for her own safety. I beg her to not further antagonize him.

"Hmm, I see the noble Mary Nighosian is among those who abandoned Amasia. I am surprised you made it this far. I would have thought wild dogs would be feasting on your carcass by now." She offers no reply. She is not afraid of our hated foe, but the safety of others in our band is of greater concern. Mother remains silent as the taunting continues.

"A swift death for the wife and son of Osigian Nighosian would be too merciful. I will enjoy watching you suffer until your bones decay under the desert sun." She stands firm as he issues a final threat. "I assure you, Mrs. Nighosian, you and the boy will never live to see Deir ez Zor or any other concentration camp."

"Sir, what do you intend to do with the two Armenians?" asks a soldier standing guard over my uncles. Sgt. Asid's eyes glare at the woman who is his sworn enemy when he gives the order, "They are the brothers of Osigian Nighosian. We will lop their heads later when the entire camp can learn what happens when you create problems for the Ottoman Empire. In the meantime, I will make sure that my sword is sharpened."

My uncles are shackled and thrown into the back of a supply truck. I may never see Varge and Ara again.

Note: The 1.5 million Armenians slaughtered by the Turkish government is said to be the first genocide of the twentieth century. Turkey continues to deny its role to attempt a systematic annihilation of an entire nation of people. (National Geographic: Rebirth of Armenia)

Chapter 15

The line is halted when the sun looms high in the sky. We are now on the down slope of the mountain. People collapse to the ground trying to capture a few minutes of rest. The water supply truck rumbles its way along the road that is strewn with more than just discarded personal effects. At times, it veers off course as the driver tries to avoid running over the bodies of those who can no longer make the journey. The truck comes to a halt near Mother and me. The corporal hands my mother a water ladle.

"You see; six ounces, just as I agreed." the corporal whispers. He looks around to be sure no other soldiers are within hearing distance. His partner discretely distributes the same quantity of water to others.

"Yes, and I shall keep my part of the agreement. Tonight, you will feast on something more palatable than bland porridge." Mother hands the ladle to me and I quickly consume the life-saving liquid. The warm water quenches my thirst for the time being, but the desert is ahead of us. I can't imagine this meager portion of water sustaining a person walking through sand in sweltering temperatures. It is useless to dwell on the matter; staying alive today is the issue.

"Come to our camp the same time as last evening," the corporal tells her. "Be careful to not alert anyone. If you are discovered, we will deny any knowledge of your existence." The two soldiers continue distributing water along the line. Mother and I remain close to the water truck to confirm that others are receiving the added proportion of water. The Turkish officers seem oblivious of the scheme to keep Armenians alive.

We have traveled eight miles since awakening and make a second stop. There is no further information about my uncles. Mother avoids any contact with the two soldiers manning the water truck during the break because the officers keep a closer watch on the deportees due to the earlier attempted escape. Yeggi appears to be having a polite conversation with the soldier who struck the deal with my mother. I hear only bits and pieces of the somewhat odd conversation.

"I once visited your shop in Amasia," the corporal informs Yeggi. "You had many fine carpets. There were wonderful weavings by Keshan, Kazak, Dagestan, Sjirvan, and others. I would say some of the nicest tapestries in the entire Ottoman Empire."

"Kind sir, you embarrass me. I was merely a simple merchant trying to serve the people."

"Come now, Mr. Yeghesian. Surely you do not expect me to believe that? I saw ornate pieces that could easily be displayed in the Sultan's palace." He pauses and adds, "That is, if the Sultan had not been deposed." Both men break into laughter at the expense of the former Ottoman ruler ousted by the Young Turks. I think something strange is going on. Yeggi would never enjoy humor about the Ottoman leader responsible for the deaths of so many Armenians. He is obviously up to something.

"It is just as I suspected," Yeggi tells the man. "You have a fine eye for quality, and now you have proved it!" He continues to satisfy the man's ego. The corporal enjoys the flattery.

"You are correct, my merchant friend. I was not always a lowly soldier, but I assume you realize that from our conversation."

"Yes, of course. No doubt you come from good stock. Perhaps there is some aristocracy in your bloodline?"

"Umm, yes, I have always believed that there might be royal blood seeping through my veins," he boasts with false modesty. Yeggi presses forward with the ego-building conversation.

"Perhaps you can check the archives in the capital to validate your family history. There are documents dating back many centuries." The suggestion causes the corporal to hesitate. He searches for a safe response to hide the fact there is no royal blood coursing through his veins. Eventually, he comes up with a story that holds some truth.

"Possibly, but many of the records have been destroyed due to centuries of turmoil throughout the land."

"Yes, that is unfortunate," Yeggi says, giving me a wink to indicate the truth has been stretched. The corporal quickly shifts the topic.

"So, I imagine your tapestry business did quite well?" he asks.

Yeggi does not have reservations about sharing his financial status. I do find this uncommon for the shrewd merchant.

"Yes, very lucrative. In fact, I had difficulty concealing all the wealth when your army plundered our village," he explains. I can't believe what our friend just shared with the enemy. The soldier's interest is peaked, and I wonder: *Has Yeggi lost his mind?*

The blare of a horn signals the end of our break, but not before the corporal makes a final comment. "The Nighosian woman will come to our camp tonight when others are asleep. Perhaps you will accompany her, and we will continue this conversation." Yeggi accepts the invitation. He is making a pact with the scoundrel, and I am baffled as to for what reason. He seems content as we walk together. There is an air of confidence when he tells me, "Do not worry, my young friend. All is well."

A bone-chilling downpour saturates our clothing following the break. The next five hours are spent shivering as we slog through mud created by the deluge. Guards walking beside us don gear to repel the downpour while others take shelter inside the vehicles that accompany this mission. The long-awaited evening arrives, and we make camp near a stream. It provides an opportunity to wash the dirt and stench from our bodies. However, the rain has made the water colder than usual. We risk hypothermia to cleanse ourselves. There is little talk; everyone is exhausted.

Mother immediately begins preparing a meal which will contain an extra quantity of food. She promised the two soldiers a tasty meal, so our dolma and kebabs will be shared. She wishes she could provide for others, but there is not enough food. There is great risk in secretly taking care of our small group. The ethnic food may be for only one night, but it is a welcomed reminder of our heritage. The meal will help satisfy an aching stomach but do little to soothe the sadness associated with tomorrow's scheduled execution.

She opens a satchel and retrieves a portion of seasoned lamb for the kebab. The meat is divided into small cubes. Some ingredients were left behind during the rushed exit from our home, but the excellent cook knows how to improvise to make the dolma. She mixes dried onions, rice, parsley, salt, pepper, and slivers of lamb into balls and then wraps them in grape leaves. There is no fresh tomato juice for the stew, but dried tomatoes simmering in water will suffice. I search the area for sticks to be used as skewers for the kebabs.

Preparation of the meal is finished. The final step is to add heat from the soldiers' campfire. The dolma and tomato stew will simmer in a pot provided by the two hosts. The skewered kebabs will have more appeal if the soldiers can be enticed to contribute potatoes and onions. We are hungry but realize the two men must be satisfied before others can partake of what remains of the meal. Mother surprises us before leaving for the rendezvous. She opens a cloth containing cookies and sets aside two for the soldiers. The remaining treats are for us. I take my time savoring the crescent cookie filled with such delicious ingredients. It is one of my favorite treats, but there will be no more during the rest of the journey.

"Mary, I will help you take this to the enemy. They are expecting me," Yeggi announces. He receives an appreciative smile for the companionship to this perilous meeting.

"I worry about you and Mr. Yeghesian meeting with the Turks," I tell my mother as they prepare to depart.

Mother believes it is too dangerous for me to accompany her and Yeggi. However, she sees my fear in being left at the camp and makes a tough decision. "Alright, you can go with us, but you will remain hidden in the bushes while we deal with these men. Is that understood?" I eagerly shake my head to agree and take Yeggi's hand for comfort as we leave our camp.

There is little talk as we make our way through the brush along the way to the Turkish campsite. I think Yeggi and my mother surely must be nervous about the encounter, but they seem to be remarkably calm. It causes me to remember something my father taught me: *We are surrounded by tragedy and heartache, but our trust remains with the Lord. Faith must truly mean believing in something one cannot see.*

~~~~~~~~~~~~~~~~~~~~~~~~~~~~~~~~

The two soldiers have a pot of boiling water ready when we near their remote camp. Yeggi makes sure that I am safely hidden before he and Mother step into the clearing. The Turkish corporal is nervously watching to make sure the two visitors are alone. The other soldier takes the food Mother has prepared. He carefully spaces the kebab skewers on rocks that encircle the fire, so the meat catches enough flame. Mother adds dried tomatoes and dolma grape leaves to the water. Yeggi and the corporal converse while the meal heats up.

"So, my friend, I am curious as to how you managed to keep your wealth a secret when you left Amasia." The corporal is intent on increasing his net worth if he can retrieve the information from our friend. It's a topic that Yeggi anticipated, and he's ready to play along.

"Hmm, it wouldn't be a secret if I told you how easy it was to fool your comrades," Yeggi replies with a sly smile.

"Ah-ha! That's good. Very good! You are a wise man, my friend." He places an arm around Yeggi's shoulder and continues to prod. "Come now, you need not fear me. Perhaps we can strike an agreement that is beneficial to both of us."

"The meal is ready," Mother informs the men. The hushed conversation is halted, but the corporal decides it is only a temporary interruption.

"Stay with me after the woman leaves. We will talk more." The corporal thinks he has the upper hand, but he has never dealt with anyone as cunning as my godfather.

~~~~~~~~~~~~~~~~~~~~~~~~~~~~

It has been at least twenty minutes since I hunkered into the bushes and strained to hear bits of the conversation while the soldiers dine on food that Mother brought to the meeting. My body begins to ache and cramp, but I dare not move about. For now, I will endure the discomfort and remain safe. Finally, the soldiers' bellies are full, and they sit around the fire sipping coffee. They appear to be pleased with the arrangement to barter water for nightly meals. Mother collects the remaining food. Yeggi rises to help her carry the goods to camp, but he meets opposition. I worry that there is going to be a problem when I see the corporal pressing his finger into Yeggi's chest. He gives a command that I have no trouble hearing from my hiding place. Yeggi has a problem.

"No, you must remain here, my merchant friend! We have much to discuss. If the woman cannot find her way back, then she too will remain here." Yeggi gives no objection as both men are holding rifles.

"I accept your kind offer of more coffee," Yeggi tells them. "You go ahead, Mary. I will join you later."

~~~~~~~~~~~~~~~~~~~~~~~~~~~~

Mother and I return to our camp and explain how we managed to get back safely thanks to Yeggi. The others in our camp are hungry and quickly share the food that she brought back. The Turks have been greedy. They devoured more of the meal than necessary, but our small group is grateful for what was salvaged. The dolma is cold, and the once healthy portions of kebabs appear meager. Any food is welcomed when one is starving.

We pray after the meal and then sleep. Yeggi does not return.

Note: Armenia had two divergent political parties during these troubled times. The Hnchak party advocated an independent socialistic Armenia. The Dashnak party proposed to fight for national liberation. Russia and Turkey sought to win alliances with both parties for control of their land. (Suny: A History of the Armenian Genocide)

Chapter 16

An alarm sounds just before dawn. This is not the usual signal that it is time to begin another day of the forced march. Soldiers are on alert rushing in all directions searching for something or someone.

I am still lying on the ground under my cover but not for long. A brazen soldier pulls me to my feet and rustles the blanket to make sure no one else is tucked under it. All the deportees are lined up and held at gunpoint while soldiers search the entire area. Whatever they are looking for is nowhere to be found.

I wonder if all this commotion has to do with Yeggi not returning last evening. My concern is put to rest when he casually walks out of the timber and joins us. He carries a glass jar filled with what appears to be milk and gives it to Arixie. She quickly prepares the life-sustaining liquid for the baby. Yeggi has accomplished what was considered impossible and he accepts no praise. Instead, he asks for a cloth to blot a trickle of blood coming from his mouth.

"Not to worry, Nishan. It is a good wound."

I am confused by the statement: *A good wound? I have never heard that saying, and Mr. Yeghesian does not seem to mind the injury. He is rather com-*

placent about all the activity throughout the campsite. It is as though he expected it.

The soldiers move on. We still don't know what it is they are trying to find. My older friend provides the answer. He shares the news that Ara and Varge escaped during the night. Sgt. Asid is livid and suspects they were aided in getting away. He announces there will be severe punishment for the troops if the two brothers are not recaptured.

I am elated that my uncles have avoided execution. Mother turns her attention to Yeggi as he bends over to spit a mixture of saliva and blood onto the ground. She uses a damp cloth to sooth the cut inside his mouth and makes a discovery.

"Yeggi, what happened to the gold teeth in the back of your mouth? They're gone!"

"Mary, there's no need to fret. A quart of milk twice per day and it only cost one gold tooth! That's a good trade." Mother appreciates the man's skillful bartering, but a question remains.

"But, Yeggi, there were *two* gold teeth."

"Oh, yes, I neglected to mention there was more to the transaction," he says casually. "The other gold tooth was traded for two very likeable young men. Now that's what I call a *great* deal!

We stand in silence admiring the man. He has truly lived up to the reputation of godfather. I prefer to think of him as a good shepherd caring for his flock. It seems appropriate to celebrate, but Yeggi suggests we pray for the safety of my uncles and the Armenian people.

This day's march begins. I am proud to walk beside a special man. He seems at peace with himself, even though we are surrounded by devastation. I worry about the fate of Ara and Varge if they are captured, so I pose a question.

"Yeggi, do you believe my uncles are going to heaven?" The wise man takes his time to respond. Then a wry smile that soothes my heart comes with his reply.

"Yes, Nishan, someday they will be in heaven... but today they're on their way to Bulgaria."

Note: In 1939, Adolf Hitler proposed to annihilate the Jewish race. He justified this heinous act by telling his commanders, "Who still talks about the extermination of the Armenians?" (Wikipedia: Did the Armenian Genocide Inspire Hitler?)

—

Chapter 17

Day four brings a huge increase in our numbers as the southward journey continues. The number of Armenian citizens being deported swells into the tens of thousands. The count would be even greater but for the masses lying along the side of the road that will never walk again. We have traveled seventy miles from Amasia and are nearing Yerevan. The large city is situated along the Hrazdan River. We are told that trucks may be there to transport the deportees the rest of the way to the camps at Aleppo and Deir ez Zor. Many believe this is just a ploy to encourage us to walk faster. Voices call out, "Why walk faster to a death camp?"

On this morning a rumor is whispered along the line. A force of freedom fighters intends to attack the Turks before we reach Yerevan. This information is bittersweet. Prior engagements to free the deportees have already claimed the lives of civilians as casualties of war.

Arixie has her hands full caring for the two children. The infant girl clings to life with the goat milk provided by the two Turkish soldiers who relish Mother's cooking. I wonder how much longer this alliance can continue before others get wise to the arrangement. Yeggi and I take turns watching over Arixie's boy. He is quite active and tends to stray when left alone.

One of the new captives in the convoy approaches us. I see the woman has nice features, but in a matter of days, fatigue and starvation will probably make her gaunt and a shell of her former self.

"Have you heard the good news?" the woman asks.

"There has been no good news since the Turks invaded our village," Mother angrily responds. "What are you referring to?"

"The Ambassador from the United States of America has been in Constantinople meeting with leaders of the Ottoman Empire." Her announcement is given cordially.

"I am sorry for being rude," Mother tells the woman. "Please tell us about the American. What does he want from the Turks?"

"His name is Henry Morgenthau. He is sympathetic toward Armenians."

"Why would the American ambassador want to help us?" Mother quizzes the woman.

She appears well-informed and recounts developments taking place in the capital city. "Ambassador Morgenthau met with Talaat and Enver Pasha. The two Turkish leaders claimed to be friendly toward the Armenians, but Morgenthau was smart enough to see through the hoax. He claims the deportation of Greeks and Armenians is a crime against humanity and should be stopped."

"Do you believe that if the United States becomes involved, there is hope we will be rescued?" my mother asks.

"Yes, I do." The woman vigorously shakes her head in the affirmative. "The Americans have been hesitant to enter the war but reports of these atrocities will surely cause them to reconsider. If the Americans join the Allied Forces, Germany and Turkey will surely be made to regret this genocide of our people." We hope the prediction comes true, but there will be no further discussion. Gunfire suddenly erupts from two different locations.

Several wounded soldiers fall to the ground as others seek refuge from the attack. Surprisingly, none of the deportees are hit by the hail of bullets. The Armenian snipers have launched the attack and are careful to identify their targets. The battle is on and we are caught in the middle. The captives rush to take cover in the ditches along the road. Mother uses her body to shield me. I see only bits and pieces of the fighting while peeking from beneath her coat.

The fact that the Armenian troops are trying to avoid endangering the captives has not gone unnoticed by the Turkish soldiers. The remaining exposed guards grab Armenian women and children as shields against the hail of incoming bullets. The snipers now risk killing the very people they intend to rescue. I press closer to my mother fearing that a stray bullet will come my way at any moment.

It seems the bloody encounter goes on for hours, but it lasts only a few minutes. There are screams coming from the deportees who are pinned down with no shelter.

I venture another look and see many of the guards lying very still on the ground. The Armenian fighters appear to be winning this battle. My elation is only temporary. The sound of vehicles moving forward from behind us indicates there are reinforcements approaching. Armored vehicles that accompany the convoy have moved to the forefront of the battle. Troop trucks are being emptied as hundreds of Turkish soldiers join the fight. Heavy artillery makes its presence known. Cannons are placed in position next to a line of mortars. Within seconds, the rock formations and trees protecting our rescuers are blown away, leaving only holes in the landscape and shredded parts of what once were human beings.

We are ordered back onto the road that is now littered with bodies of Armenians and Turks. They were enemies just minutes earlier; now they share common ground. We bow our heads as we pass the spot where the Armenian soldiers gave their lives attempting to save us. They were brave men and women who sacrificed for something called freedom.

Note: U.S. Ambassador Henry Morgenthau's quote regarding Turkish leaders: "My failure to stop the destruction of the Armenians made Turkey for me a place of horror. I found intolerable my further daily association with men who were still reeking with the blood of nearly one million Armenians." (AGBU: Ambassador Morgenthau's Story)

Chapter 18

Day six is a travesty. It begins with Sgt. Asid in a rage because the convoy is not moving fast enough. We now average only fourteen miles per day since evacuating Amasia. Many of our people are exhausted and can barely place one foot ahead of the other. We reached Yerevan yesterday and, as suspected, there were no vehicles to transport us. Now the sergeant tells us that there is a schedule to keep which requires no less than twenty-five miles per day. He says it is needed to intersect another caravan of deportees. Thousands of captives will be separated into two groups at the rendezvous point. Some will go south to the Deir ez Zor camp while others will move westward to the Aleppo desert. This sad news may splinter generations of family members.

"I have been tolerant with you lazy people as you ambled through the mountain, and now you continue to drag your feet." He elects to ignore the fact that those he chooses to call 'lazy' are starving children or elderly. "Today, I put an end to your meandering. One of your people will be sacrificed each day for every mile you fail to reach the number twenty-five." He punctuates the decree by drawing his sword from the scabbard and waving it above his head. "I will personally carry out the executions!"

"We are Sgt. Asid's turnips," Yeggi says under his breath. I quiz him about the odd comment. "Nishan, it is an old saying. No matter how hard you squeeze a turnip, it will not yield blood. The people are old and sick. They have lost their spirit and have nothing more to give. Squeeze them as much as you can, and they still cannot walk any faster." I realize the sergeant's preposterous demand is a travesty, and more heartache is yet to come.

We camp close to the Hrazdan River. The beautiful waterway gives hope that we can satisfy our thirst and bathe. The Turks see it as an opportunity to inflict more torture when they forbid us to access the water. Instead, we are held at bay and made to watch the soldiers frolic in the river. They wash their uniforms in the water while mocking the people whose clothes and bodies are covered in dried mud.

Arixie rests against a tree. The baby girl is not doing well. Her breathing is shallow, and she now rejects the milk we presumed would save her life. Mother comforts Arixie as Yeggi attends to the baby.

"I'm afraid there is nothing we can do for the child," he sadly reports. I ask him if this means the baby will die. His answer is steeped in faith. "Some things must be left for the Lord to decide."

The focus on the baby's well-being draws attention away from Arixie's toddler. The little boy seizes the opportunity to scoot to the river bank. Soon thereafter, we hear shouts coming from where soldiers are bathing. The raucous noise brings a realization that the boy is missing. Yeggi leaves to investigate and finds that our worst fears are realized. The little fellow wandered too close to the monsters that have no respect for human life. They held the boy underwater and wagered how long he would struggle. The murderers show no regret as they raise the tiny corpse above their heads and shout, "This is what happens to Armenians who do not accept Islam!" I do not understand this manner of thinking. A child is slaughtered for amusement. These are butchers, and we are the lambs.

Arixie is despondent when given the news that her son has been killed. Her eyes glaze over as she stares into space. The only thing that might console her grief is the baby, and now the infant closes her eyes for the last time.

There are no words to describe the heartache of losing two lovely children in the same day. I cry for Arixie, the kind lady who brings so much joy to my life. Perhaps I will never again feel her daily hug or hear her tell me, "Nishan, you are a good boy. I love you like a son."

Now, she slumps against a tree and expresses no self-worth. "I have lost everything. There is nothing left in my life."

Mother refuses to stand by and allow her close friend to surrender all hope for a future. I listen intently as she grasps Arixie's hand and looks into her eyes. "Arixie, you *do* have more to live for. Our people need you, especially during these troubled times." Mother doesn't give up. "You are an inspiration to everyone. People on this journey see your fortitude and gather strength to endure another day. You are important to all of us."

Arixie listens but remains despondent. "Mary, my life is empty without the children."

I think even my mother's impassioned plea cannot save our friend. "Your little ones are now safe with the Lord, but you will have more children. They will be as gracious and as beautiful as their mother."

"You really believe this will happen?" A sparkle of hope shows in our friend's eyes.

"Yes, with all my heart," Mother answers and hugs the lady. "There will be at least three beautiful children with the spirit of their mother." The two women continue to hold one another.

"Yes, three children would be very nice." Arixie murmurs.

"And, what will you name the little Armenians?" Mother asks, now realizing the conversation is having the desired effect.

"One of the daughters will be called Anna, and a son will be named Noray. I'm not sure about the other daughter," she says, looking to her friend for advice.

113

"Vartanoush," Mother answers without hesitation. Arixie's facial expression tells me it is the perfect name. She always refers to the baby as her sweet rose, and now the prospect of having a new daughter named for a scented rose brings joy to her heart. My mother has turned a sad event into a promise of hope.

Later, I tell her how special she is for saving a lost soul. She graciously replies, "My friend would do the same for me."

Note: The Sultan of the Ottoman Empire formed a Cossack-like militia called Hamidiye to carry out raids on villages and steal Armenian properties. These murderous Kurdish bandits committed their atrocities under the protection of the Sultan. (Suny: History of the Armenian Genocide)

Chapter 19

A few days later, we are south of Yerevan when an incident occurs that changes our lives. The forced march is halted as we come upon a vehicle bearing medical insignia stopped on the side of the road.

A Turkish army officer is kneeling on the ground holding a woman in his arms. He calls for assistance to help with the ailing lady. We welcome the rest stop as Sgt. Asid investigates the situation. Shortly thereafter, he motions to have my mother escorted to the scene. No one prevents me from tagging along. We reach the vehicle and see that the woman lying on the ground has her eyes closed and is not moving. The man aiding her wears the uniform of a lieutenant in the medical corps. Mother instructs me to stand back as she kneels beside the officer.

"She is my Armenian housekeeper," he says softly, "and she is dying." There is nothing that can be done for the woman in her final moments. The officer makes a compassionate plea, "Please comfort her." Mother gently caresses the woman's hand and her eyes slightly open. I expect to see the weariness that so many of our people show from torture and degradation. This women's look is peaceful, as though she accepts her fate.

"Heevant yem. Surb mard?" she tells Mother in a weak voice. I understand her message that she is in poor health and ready to have a holy man administer the rites.

"Amen ench lav e." Mother tells her 'everything is fine' and a pleasing smile comes over the face of the woman who is near death. The two women share an intimate conversation with their native language before the lady closes her eyes for the last time.

This moment brings something unexpected. I am surprised the doctor's eyes fill with tears. Never have I seen a Turkish officer grieving on behalf of an Armenian. I am witnessing the humanity of a medical person rather than a soldier of the Ottoman Empire.

"It is time to move on!" Sgt. Asid demands. His patience is exhausted due to the delay. "We need not waste any more daylight on a dead person!" The medical lieutenant takes issue with the crude remark.

"We will bury her first, and then you may proceed with your clandestine mission," he tells the sergeant. I sense the lieutenant is not an advocate of the forced deportation. Sgt. Asid flashes an indignant sneer but dares not challenge the doctor's military rank. He begrudgingly orders the two soldiers in the water truck to grab shovels for a grave. The captive deportees relish the additional time to rest. A meaningful conversation takes place.

"Thank you for being with us during this difficult time," the lieutenant tells Mother. "She was a great help to me at my home in Constantinople."

"You are most welcome, and I thank you for respecting her," Mother replies. "She spoke kindly of you during those final moments." The man shows his appreciation with a nod that seems to say the lady was more than a servant.

"She was a good cook; housekeeper and she was..." he pauses to search for the right words. Then something strange happens when he elects to finish his sentence while speaking Armenian. *"Paregamoohees e."* I am shocked! Did this soldier of the Ottoman Empire just tell us that the dying lady is his friend? And, how is it that he speaks Armenian so fluently? This man is unique.

I know the lieutenant could be chastised for admitting he has befriended someone considered to be the enemy. I wonder why he appears to be so different from the others who hold us in bondage. Mother is also curious.

"Sir, my name is Mary Nighosian, and this is my son, Nishan. I keep an organized household and have been told that I am an excellent cook." He shows interest, but before he can respond, the corporal working on the gravesite interrupts. He is concerned about losing the person who lately provides his good meals.

"I caution the lieutenant to be leery of this woman," the corporal advises. "Her food may give you a bellyache." He and the other soldier share a

117

laugh, but the lieutenant is not fooled. He thinks something is amiss and challenges the soldier.

"Tell me, corporal, how is it that you are able to assess this lady's talents with cuisine?" The man is befuddled by the sophisticated language and fears stumbling into a trap. If he confesses to bartering water and other goods in return for Mother's cooking, there will be severe consequences. It is best to terminate the arrangement and eliminate what is now a liability to him. There is a quick reversal as he assails her exceptional talent with food.

"My apologies, sir. I was merely speaking in generalities and have no actual knowledge of the woman's abilities." We remain silent as the situation plays out.

"Then, corporal, I suggest you continue digging and leave the decisions to me." Heretofore, I considered the lieutenant rather mild-mannered, but his next comment tells me he is quite capable of asserting himself. "You men work a little faster, or there may be two more graves for someone else to dig." Both men give a swift salute and put their shovels to good use.

"Thank you, sir. That man has little knowledge of my true abilities," Mother tells the lieutenant. He understands and continues the conversation.

"Madam, I am interested in securing your services at my home. I can offer food, shelter, clothing and a safe environment." This generous offer is enticing, but Mother is unsure if I am included. She steps aside to let the officer get a better look at me. I am nervous and anticipate rejection.

"I believe your traveling companion is quite handsome," he says with a smile.

"Sir, he is strong for his age and quite familiar with doing chores." I worry that this is not a strong case for accepting me as part of the arrangement. "He is all I have left now that my husband is gone." The lieutenant understands her meaning and keeps the conversation cordial.

"Mary, of course the boy will come with you. Keeping family together is important." He removes a leather glove and steps forward to offer me his hand. His grip is nothing as I imagined from an Ottoman soldier. The hand is soft, much as one might expect from a refined gentleman. "Hello, Nishan, I am Dr. Demirr. You are welcome in my home."

This is all so strange. Ten minutes ago, Mother and I were trudging toward an enemy concentration camp in the desert. By a stroke of luck, we are now offered freedom. I am elated, but she is concerned.

"Sir, my son and I are truly grateful, but we travel with close friends. It would be difficult to leave them behind." This plea for Arixie and Mr. Yeghesian becomes awkward.

"I am sorry, Mary, but it will be looked upon as an act of treason if I were to grant such a request. I can justify the two of you, but my superiors already believe I am too lenient in my thinking. It could even jeopardize your opportunity."

My mother must now make a heart-wrenching decision between friendship and freedom. "I understand," she tells the lieutenant. "May I speak with our friends?"

"Yes, you are welcome to confer with them. I will await your decision."

We start to return to the line, but Sgt. Asid intercedes. Mother informs him we have permission to speak with friends regarding abandoning the march. He is aware officers are allowed to engage Armenians as domestic helpers, and attempting to prevent her from leaving is not an option. That may not be the same when it comes to considering me.

"Not the boy!" Sgt. Asid yells to the lieutenant. "He goes to Deir ez Zor or Aleppo with the rest of the prisoners!" The officer lets the enlisted man know he does not appreciate the terminology.

"Sergeant, I believe you meant to say Armenians!" The sergeant rolls his eyes in frustration. He has little respect for an officer who has not engaged in battle.

"Armenians, prisoners, deportees; the words are different but they're all the same to me," the sergeant growls. He begrudgingly concedes. "Fine, have it your way. Take the woman *and* the boy. I am happy to be rid of Osigian Nighosian's wife and son." He approaches me before exiting. His hand grips the sword in a threatening manner. It is a frightening moment when he sneers at me and leans close to my face. The hideous scars cannot be hidden by his dirty beard. I say nothing even when his mangled nose is inches from my face. He is trying to incite me to retaliate, but the travesties of recent days have taught me to stand firm. I glare at Sgt. Asid to let him know I am not intimidated. He brushes past me and shouts a final insult, "Humph, a prince of Armenia? All I see is the last of the Armenians."

Mother and I approach Arixie and Yeggi. They listen intently to what the lieutenant has offered. Emotions tug at each person's heart. I believe my mother will never leave her lifelong friend. The lieutenant and his driver are patiently waiting, but our time is gone. Sgt. Asid orders the deportees to move out. Only one person is willing to make what may be a life and death decision.

"You must go," Arixie says with tears pooling in her eyes. Yeggi turns away and looks into a distant sky. There is no mistaking the message. He shakes his head to show he agrees with Arixie. I move to Yeggi's side and take his hand. He tries to maintain his composure so as not to alarm me, but tears betray him.

"I am sorry that you see me this way, my young friend." He uses the sleeve of his shirt to wipe away the tears. This man I admire so much bares his soul to me. "Nishan, I am filled with sadness, joy, and love all at the same moment." He turns to Mother, "Mary, this is the right decision. Do it not for yourself, but for all of us." He points toward the endless convoy of suffering people. "You and the boy will carry on their legacy."

Mother graciously accepts the decision. There is a sorrowful goodbye to the dear friends. I put my arms around the man who has been like a grandfather to me. "I love you, Mr. Yeghesian, and I will never forget you." His gentle hand strokes the back of my head as he leans over to whisper a farewell.

"Take care of your mother, Nishan. You will always be in my thoughts and prayers."

~~~~~~~~~~~~~~~~~~~~~~~~~~~~

We are seated with Dr. Demir in the rear seat of the medical vehicle. The driver pulls onto the road. He is careful to avoid hitting any of the poor souls as we drive past the human convoy. Hundreds of gaunt faces stare aimlessly trying to peer through the darkened glass windows. Their emaciated bodies can barely put one foot ahead of the other. These words will live forever in my memory: *But, for the grace of God, there go I.*

Note: In 1915, Armenian villagers wage a historic battle for 53 days against the Turkish Army on the Mountain Musa Dagh. Outmanned, outgunned, and lacking supplies, the surviving valiant warriors are finally rescued by a French warship joined by other Allied ships. (Wikipedia: Forty Days at Musa Dagh)

Chapter 20

Mother and I are traveling in a vehicle accompanied by a medical doctor who is a lieutenant in the Turkish army. We know little about this man other than he may have saved our lives by offering freedom from the forced march to a concentration camp.

We are informed that it is not necessary to refer to the doctor by his military rank. "The military is not my career," he tells us. "Medical service is my true profession."

We are headed to his home in the port city of Constantinople located on an eastern border of the Ottoman Empire. It is a major city and currently the political hub of the Turkish government. Every major decision regarding Turkey's involvement in the current world war comes out of this city. Mother and I will be surrounded by Islamic Turks who hate Christian Armenians: *Perhaps my thoughts about having been saved are premature.*

The final leg of the trip to Constantinople is not easy, even if it is in motorized transportation. The terrain is rough and challenging for the vehicle as its hard tires bounce through ditches, over rocks, and weave around disabled military equipment. This mode of transportation is uncommon to me. I have never ridden in a vehicle which contains two rear seats facing one another. Dr. Demirr is seated in the last seat. We face him with our backs to the driver. Our host engages in conversation as we ramble toward our destination. I remain a silent listener.

"Tell me about your life in Amasia before the deportation, Mary." The awkward term delays a response. It is a haunting reminder of the Turks' deception to the free world. Mother is cautious not to damage the relationship with our new benefactor.

"Sir, the family was engaged in agriculture. The acreage produced fruits, vegetables, and grains which helped to sustain the population of our village." She hesitates and solemnly adds, "Now, that is all gone."

"I'm sorry for your loss, Mary. This war has been hurtful to many innocent people," the doctor says in a saddened tone. It is as though he reflects on something personal, but there is no elaboration and he shifts the topic. "Perhaps we should discuss your duties in the household."

"Yes, sir, I wish to know your expectation of me," she politely responds and places a finger to her lips reminding me to remain quiet.

"Your initial responsibilities will involve preparation of a morning and noon meal for me and a staff of four personnel assigned to a medical unit adjacent to my domicile." Mother sees my confused look and defines the unfamiliar term.

"Domicile means his home, Nishan," she gives a smile and returns her attention to the man as he continues to describe our new surroundings.

"The medical unit has a dual purpose. It not only serves as a facility to conduct examinations for troops being entered to the military, but it also aids those who are recovering from injuries. The military hospitals in the capital city are filled now that the Allied forces have intensified the war in Turkey." I pay close attention to the conversation, knowing that the outcome of this war he refers to may determine our future. "You will also be responsible for maintaining a clean, well-organized household. Occasionally, I am called upon to entertain dignitaries, government officials, and ranking military officers as they go about their business seemingly trying to make sense out of all this human tragedy which surrounds us." The man is upset with himself for choosing to make a political statement to an audience consisting of a newly-acquired housekeeper and her son. "I apologize, Mary. You and the boy need not listen to me rant about world affairs."

"Yes, I understand." Mother's accommodating reply brings an unexpected response.

"I'm glad *you* do, Mary, because I certainly can't wrap my thoughts around how half the people in the world can hate the other half to the point of killing one another on battlefields. Does that make sense to you?"

"No, sir, it does not."

"Humph. Lately I've been in the field patching up soldiers so much I may have a touch of battle fatigue myself." He brushes his fingers through a full head of hair. The thick brown locks are showing a few strands of grey, perhaps a sign this man has already endured a lifetime beyond his youthful years. He gazes out the window of our vehicle, and for a few moments, his thoughts are somewhere far, far away. Mother and I sit quietly and barely hear him whisper to himself, "It will be nice to be home in Constantinople."

Later, the doctor gives further details regarding Mother's work in the home and at the medical unit. He explains that as she becomes more familiar with the surroundings, there may be added responsibilities. I gather the lady who died by the roadside was a trusted assistant. "Everyone helps out when it comes to saving lives. There's no time to check on the color of someone's skin, their nationality, or station in life," he tells us. His comment tells me more about this man who has befriended us: *Yes, this is an unusual man. He appears to be thoughtful, deep, and even a bit mysterious. I wonder if he's too good to be true.*

The discussion has been interesting, but now our host surprises me. "Nishan, I am sorry if I seem to ignore you. You are welcome to speak up."

I am caught off-guard and look to my mother for guidance. She gives me a confident look, so I nervously blurt out, "Oh, that's okay. I enjoy listening to you talk." It is a silly response, but the doctor overlooks my embarrassment and continues to engage me in conversation.

"I am interested in your schooling. Can you read and write?"

"Yes, sir. The people at the Armenian school in our village were good at teaching us the letters and numbers. Also, my mother reads to me from the Holy Scriptures every night." I see her frown and realize that perhaps too much information has been shared. She tries to make amends.

"Forgive him, sir, he doesn't..."

Dr. Demirr raises his hand to stop Mother in mid-sentence. "You need not apologize, Mary. I understand your concern. Yes, you and the boy will be residing in Constantinople among many who have a different belief from Christianity. For your own sake, be cautious when and where you profess your vows."

The rough road makes for a bumpy ride, but it is a welcome change from the agony of Sgt. Asid's death march. Some of our frequent stops are merely to ward off nausea while others allow our driver to keep the motor from overheating and to check for cracks in the hard rubber tires.

We come to a village just before nightfall and stop at a farmhouse. Mother and I accompany the doctor to the front door. It has been several days since we have slept in a bed, and we soon learn that the anticipated comfort is not to be.

The homeowner is willing to accommodate Dr. Demirr and his driver, but he poses a strong objection as he gives a nasty look to a mother and son.

"They are Armenians?" the man asks.

"Yes, part of the entourage traveling with me," the doctor replies in a self-assured manner.

"It makes no difference. I allow no Armenians to enter my home."

"I accept responsibility for the woman and boy." The man is not pleased but decides not to further challenge a uniformed officer of the Ottoman Empire.

"They can sleep in the barn!" he shouts angrily and points to a shabby building some fifty yards away. The leaning structure is missing much of its framework. My anger for such degrading treatment would have spilled forth a few weeks ago, but now I am accustomed to the verbal cruelty that comes from those who consider themselves superior to others. Cruelty coming from the Turkish guards on the march taught me that to lash out only gives satisfaction to the oppressor. Now the homeowner is wavering, so the doctor takes a different approach.

"If these people are not allowed in your house, then I expect you to provide a decent meal, bathing facilities, and a change of clothing for them," he demands. "Otherwise, you will forfeit the stipend the army provides for using your home."

The homeowner is not pleased with the arrangement, but the extra money is a strong motivator. Greed makes him a reluctant host. Mother and I walk to the rundown building and hope it will remain standing until daybreak. Our beds are rickety cots most likely discarded by the army. The 'bathing facility' is a spicket of trickling water used to fill the animal trough. Our meal consists of a few slices of bread and cheese. Mother is given a well-worn dress and I receive trousers. A length of rope from the barn helps cinch the oversized garment around my waist. Yes, the situation is poor, but Mother instructs me to not complain. She tells me the doctor has done all he can to help us. On this night, we share accommodations with an ox and three goats.

The driver, Cpl. Armond, is a welcomed sight the next morning. He brings cooked eggs and other food that we have not touched since abandoning Amasia. Now, such things as food, water, clothing and shelter are simple pleasures I shall never again take for granted. He sees the deplorable conditions we suffered during the night and promises to report it to his lieutenant.

We meet at the medical vehicle half an hour later to begin the day's trip. The homeowner does not speak nor look at us. Instead, he makes it a point to spit on the ground as our vehicle passes him. When we are miles down the road, we learn from the corporal that Dr. Demirr reduced the man's lodging stipend by half because of the conditions we endured. Mother tells me how we can thank the doctor. "We will show our appreciation

by working hard for him once we reach Constantinople."

Note: Armenians were known for their thrift. They pros-
pered in many other locations beginning with the 1870's.
They were prominent in urban trades, crafts, finance, and
international commerce. Armenian emigrants to America
and Europe sent home their savings which enabled those in
Armenia to buy land and farm machines. (Suny: History of
the Armenian Genocide)

Chapter 21

The morning drive is filled with interesting conversation as Dr. Demirr and Mother discuss in greater detail the aspects of her work in his home. At times, he shifts the conversation away from household duties and launches into more colorful commentary that causes me to listen more intently. I latch onto every word as the learned man describes a city that years earlier accommodated only small fishing boats and a few passenger ships.

"Nishan, today the harbor anchors battleships, troop carriers, and vessels laden with cargo of trucks, cannons, and other military weapons of destruction." His tone tells me that he prefers the peaceful seaport that faded into history with the outbreak of war. I wonder what is in store for an Armenian woman and her son who come from a village hundreds of miles away.

The first hours pass quickly as our vehicle makes good time despite the pitfalls along the road. Armond avoids conversation except on occasions when the doctor addresses him. He appears content with his role in transporting the medical officer to assignments. A rifle resting against the front seat reminds me he is also charged with protecting his lieutenant.

It is only when we round a curve running adjacent to a grove of timber that our leisure ride is interrupted. A troop transport truck is disabled in the middle of the road. It is being used for cover by soldiers under assault by gunfire coming from the woods. Armond slams on the brakes to avoid hitting the wrecked vehicle and our automobile skids sideways. He manages to keep the vehicle upright as we slide closer to the center of the battle. It is a harrowing experience with mud and loose rock flying everywhere until we slam into a ditch on the side of the road.

"Is everyone okay?" Armond calls out.

"Yes, I believe we are all in one piece," Dr. Demirr responds after checking Mother and me for injuries. The uncontrolled slide sent the three of us in the rear seats sprawling to the floor. A few bruises are the extent of our injuries; however, any relief that accompanies knowing we are all safe is quickly dashed.

Ping! Ping!

Two bullets strike the side of the car.

Ping!

A third shot shatters a side window and sends shards of glass into the vehicle.

Armond grabs the rifle from the front seat and dives out of the vehicle. He shouts instructions to us. "The door is unlatched. I will give you cover while you get out on this side of the car!" He fires several rounds, and Dr. Demirr kicks the door open. We hurriedly slither from the vehicle into the ditch.

It gives us safety, but one of the bullets hits the corporal. He drops to the ground clutching his leg. Dr. Demirr rushes to aid the wounded driver. Fortunately, it is only a flesh wound from a ricochet, but Cpl. Armond is no longer in the battle. Mother tells me to keep my head down, along with another piece of important information. "They are probably Armenian freedom fighters," she whispers for my ears only.

Dr. Demirr temporarily sheds the role of a medical healer and draws his pistol from the holster. He fires several shots in the direction of the timber.

War perplexes me: *Today, my life could end at the hands of people who are fighting to free my nation from tyranny, yet, I may be saved by a Turkish lieutenant who is risking his life to protect me. War is very complex and neither side is a true winner.*

The reason for the gunfire becomes obvious as we huddle together and observe that the main target of the attack is a Turkish patrol a short distance ahead of us. Wounded soldiers are stranded along the ditch as their comrades wage a battle against an unseen enemy. Cries of pain come from men in need of medical attention. Bullets are flying in all directions. I am surprised to see the doctor expose himself when he returns to our vehicle. He reaches inside to retrieve a medical satchel and quickly makes his way back to us amid a hail of gunfire. The soldiers in the Turkish patrol send up a cheer for the brave lieutenant as he crawls to their wounded comrades. It's a deadly situation, but when Mother sees the man desperately giving aid to each disabled soldier, she decides to act.

"Stay behind the vehicle with our wounded driver, Nishan." She leaves me and makes her way along the ditch to join the doctor. Armond and I watch as she exposes herself to danger for the sake of others. Dr. Demirr instructs Mother to apply pressure to a soldier's wound while he tends to others. The shooting slows down, and I disregard my mother's instructions. I am on my belly crawling to her location.

"Nishan, shame on you! You should have stayed put," she scolds.

Our medical friend takes time to look up from tending to a soldier and shouts support in my favor. "Mary, I think the boy is safer with us. This is no time to quibble over where we may get shot." His attention returns to the business at hand. "I need your help over here! Bring more bandages!" Mother hurries to the doctor's side.

The shooting becomes sporadic, and a sergeant leading the Turkish patrol makes his way to our location. "We were headed back to our base camp when they ambushed us. We are way overdue, so reinforcements should be here soon." The doctor is busy trying to save lives, so he dispenses with returning the sergeant's salute.

"We are lucky you came along, sir. These men may not have made it if it were not for you and your assistant." The reference to Mother gives me a sense of pride. Dr. Demirr lets the compliment stand. He is applying a tourniquet to slow the bleeding from a soldier's severed artery. Informing the sergeant that my mother is merely a newly-acquired housekeeper is not a priority. "Sir, do you have any orders for me?" the sergeant asks.

The doctor continues to work on the wounded soldier, but the question seems to trigger a bit of humor. His response comes with a slight smile. "Yes, sergeant, I do have an order for you. Tell your men to keep their heads down and try not to get shot." It takes a moment, but the sergeant comes to realize he has been given good advice under the circumstances. Dr. Demirr seems to be a man disgusted with war and the heartache it brings. His final comment to the patrol leader clearly states his position. "Now, if you don't mind, sergeant, I will return to what I have been trained to do, and I assure you it is not killing people."

The shooting slows to only a few shots, and the sergeant believes the Armenians who attacked his patrol may be vacating the timber. Mother continues to assist with treating wounded soldiers. The supplies in the medical kit are rapidly dwindling.

"I'm afraid some of these men won't make it if we can't get more medical supplies," Dr. Demirr tells us as he moves to another wounded soldier.

My only involvement has been to keep my head down and stay out of the way, but now she calls to me. "Nishan, you can help, but you must follow my instructions. Do you understand me?"

"Yes, I will do exactly as you tell me."

135

"There are more medical supplies in our vehicle. I want you to crawl along the ditch and tell Cpl. Armond to get you those supplies. Bring them here as quickly as you can. Keep your head down and do not expose yourself to the gunfire." She pulls me closer. It hurts to see tears in her eyes. I am her only child and she is sending me into danger. I understand the deep meaning when she says, "I love you, Nishan. Come back to me safe." She gives me a kiss and sends me on the mission.

I slither into the ditch, hesitating only long enough to see the worried look on my mother's face. I follow her instructions, staying low in the ditch to remain hidden from the people shooting at us. The urgency of the moment sends blood rushing through my body. The feeling is strangely familiar as I recall participating in an adventure that cost the lives of two good friends. This is no game; there is no joy in life and death situations.

No shots come in my direction. I make my way to where Cpl. Armond is resting behind the heavy frame of the medical vehicle. He disregards the flesh wound to his leg and retrieves the extra medical supplies from a storage compartment in the vehicle. A piece of advice comes when he hands me the needed supplies. "Be careful, Nishan. The bullets coming at you do not know if you are Turkish or Armenian."

The difficulty on the return trip is compounded as I lie on my side and inch forward while balancing the bundle of medical supplies on one hip. It is awkward, but at least there is only a scattering of shots being fired. It seems much longer, but the mission is accomplished in a matter of minutes, much to the relief of my mother. Dr. Demirr spends the next half-hour using the additional supplies to treat the remaining soldiers. The shooting ends and there is prolonged stillness. The sergeant leads his able-bodied men in a search of the timber and confirms the attackers vacated the area. Reinforcements arrive, and Cpl. Armond joins the other wounded soldiers for the trip to a field hospital. Our medical vehicle sustained damage but survived the attack. Five bullet holes and a shattered window equal the extent of damage. The engine is in running condition. One of the soldiers from the patrol serves as our temporary driver to Constantinople.

The final leg of the journey provides time to reflect on this most recent episode. There was enough evidence left in the timber to confirm the attack was initiated by Armenian troops fighting to free our country from tyranny. My involvement was spirited with a sense of compassion for the Turkish soldiers who were suffering. Nevertheless, I aided the enemy.

Note: In 1903, Czar Nicholas II ordered confiscation of Armenian properties in Russia. The Armenians rebelled and on January 9, 1905, Russian soldiers fired on a peaceful demonstration by Armenians in St. Petersburg, killing dozens. It became known as 'Bloody Sunday'. Russia abandoned the Armenians and used its police and army to crush the Armenian freedom movement. (Suny: History of the Armenian Genocide)

Chapter 22

Early 1916

Mother and I made it to Constantinople to live in Dr. Demirr's home. It was one month ago that we were rescued from the death march. The home is impressive, built of native stone and standing three stories high overlooking the harbor that opens into the Mediterranean Sea. There are storage buildings and a large garage for multiple vehicles at the rear of the property. Level one contains a banquet hall and adjoining meeting rooms. A second tier gets the most use as much of the daily activity is conducted here. It also houses the doctor's study and medical library. He spends a good deal of time in this quiet place. In fact, I believe he even sleeps there at night. This seems odd to me.

As for the third floor, I have little knowledge other than it contains bedrooms which are no longer used. I find it strange that there are portraits of Dr. Demirr with an attractive woman and two children, but they are not present in the house. In the time we have been here, I have never seen anyone other than Cpl. Armond go to the third level, not even Dr. Demirr. I occasionally come upon indications that a family has resided in the home. Sometimes it is a wayward toy that perhaps rolled under an ottoman or a child's open storybook waiting to be finished later.

I ask Cpl. Armond about the third floor. His response is rather evasive: "It is closed off for good reason."

Reports come forth that more than one million Armenians have either perished or disappeared at the hands of the Ottoman Turks during the past two years. We hear nothing regarding our friends, Arixie and Yeggi.

What is called a world war rages on with Axis and Allied powers splitting the entire European and Asian continents. Germany, Bulgaria, Austria-Hungary, and the Ottoman Empire battle Great Britain, France, Russia, Italy, and Belgium on multiple fronts. The Allies continue to urge the United States of America to enter the fray, but the young country created only 140 years earlier is hesitant to engage in world conflict.

Constantinople is filled with activity. The population swells as government officials and high-ranking military personnel settle their families in the capital city. The war edges closer to a climax.

The threat to blockade the harbor of this port city by British and French ships becomes more of a reality each day. I would find Constantinople to be a magnificent city were it not for the sickening sight and smell of war throughout the streets. The city beckons one to appreciate its centuries-old mansions lining the cliffs overlooking the harbor.

Mother and I sleep in one of these impressive structures every night thanks to the good doctor. She told me that not so many years ago, people moved about freely through the markets filled with imported merchandise and foods from many countries. The streets of Constantinople were crowded with shoppers representing varied ethnic groups that at least tolerated one another.

Today, Constantinople is different. There are more persons in uniform on the streets than those in casual attire. Army and Navy personnel representing various countries occupy government buildings, and Turkish police (gendarmes) are constantly watching for persons who infiltrate the city to become stowaways on a ship leaving the port. There is danger in the streets, so it is a rare occasion when I can leave the protection of the doctor's residence.

It is an unusual living arrangement. The spacious grounds of the home are adjacent to a medical unit that cares for wounded soldiers and examines troops being mustered into service. Dr. Demirr and the other physicians make the final decision whether a recruit is fit to serve. The war has taken a tremendous toll on the Ottoman Empire. Those currently being pressed into action were just boys not many years ago.

The home we live in is magnificent to the point that it is occasionally used for receptions and other special events. The Ottoman leaders believe that utilizing the doctor's home is less threatening to dignitaries from other countries when they visit the capital city on official business. The high ceilings, draped tapestries, and highly-polished marble floors remind me of the mansions in the stories my father used to tell about the Ottoman royalty of earlier centuries. Today, much of that history has been soiled due to the current regime led by Enver, Talaat, and Djemal Pasha.

The rooms where Mother and I sleep may not be as stunning as other parts of the residence, but they are nicer than anything we have been used to. Dr. Demirr shows none of the trappings usually connected with persons of wealth in this city. There is a contradiction associated with this city that makes no sense to me. Commerce within the Ottoman Empire is being destroyed due to the war, but the affluent class continues to flaunt their riches. Dr. Demirr gives no outward indication that he comes from aristocracy, but it is known by those in power. He is a usual guest at receptions dealing with matters of state. The man remains pleasant, although he is careful to not become overly friendly with the household and medical center staff. I think it has something to do with avoiding the perception that he is too sympathetic to non-Turkish people.

Mother oversees the cooking and housekeeping at the residence. The transition from the woman who died by the roadside is smooth. The lady was organized and efficient, just like Mother. I believe it is no coincidence that both women share the Armenian traits.

The permanent staff consists of my mother, a gardener named Ishmail, Cpl. Armond and two other workers who do not reside in the house. They arrive daily to carry out varied activities in maintaining the home. Additional people join to help when the doctor hosts an event. My fascination with the marble pillars and floors leads Dr. Demirr to believe I can lend a hand with maintaining the sprawling home. I enthusiastically polish the marble and dust the rooms three days a week and help the gardener on two other days. A sixth day is my favorite because I am assigned to Armond. He brings some joy into my life telling stories as we go about maintaining and polishing the doctor's military and personal vehicles. I learn a great deal about Dr. Demirr from the corporal, but he never gossips about the man he serves and protects.

"Armond, how long have you been with the doctor?" I ask as we casually polish the smooth fenders of a 1914 French Renault.

"I have served Lieutenant Demirr since 1913," the corporal answers, respecting his superior's military rank. "We both entered the military in the same year. I enlisted, but he had no choice." I am eager to learn much more, and it comes immediately after Armond loads his cloth with another glob of wax.

"The war was expanding beyond the Ottoman borders and I took it as an opportunity to follow my destiny. I was born into a military family," Armond tells me as he adds a bit of spit to help spread the wax onto the Renault. "My father and grandfather were military men. My ancestors may even have fought against the crusaders during the Holy Wars centuries ago." I give a suspicious look and Armond recants the story. "Of course, there is also the possibility that a few relatives were thieves and scoundrels." He gives me a wink and we break into laughter. The gaiety is cut short when the affable corporal grimaces from the leg wound not fully healed. I hold my questions until the pain subsides.

"How did the doctor get into the army if he didn't enlist?" I ask as our buffing brings a bright shine to the vehicle. Armond takes a step back to admire our work. Now satisfied that the buffing has produced a bright shine on the pricey Renault, he proceeds to answer my question.

"Dr. Demirr was a medical student when the war broke out. He was called to military duty but given the option of a deferment for one year to finish medical school. The alternative was to move to the front lines and perhaps never return. You might say it was a matter of put down the scalpel and pick up a rifle." I understand the bit of humor, but I am more interested in the rest of the story, especially when Armond continues. "So, the medical student stayed in school to become the good physician that we know. It's too bad it had to come at such a high price."

"And, that was?"

"He was obligated to four years servitude as an officer in the Army of the Ottoman Empire. It came at a time when doctors were called upon to treat thousands of wounded and dying soldiers." The story intrigues me and I want to know more.

"Is that what you mean when you say it came with a high cost?"

"No, not at all. Our doctor paid a much more ultimate price for his service to the country. I prefer not to talk about it any further today." It is obvious we are finished with the sensitive topic, so I shift to another question.

"Do you think the doctor will remain in the military after the war?" Armond gives me a look as if it is not even worth answering.

"Of course not, silly boy. Why would he? He comes from a wealthy family. My goodness, he can easily live out his lifetime without acquiring more wealth."

"What about you, Armond? Will you stay with the doctor when he leaves the military?"

"Probaby not, my inquisitive friend." It is the first time he has called me a friend, and I like it. "I already told you that I am a career soldier. I will be promoted to the rank of sergeant and command troops in battle. Most likely I will die unless this filthy war ends soon." I believe Armond has a fatal but realistic view about life. He tells me there is more work to be completed, so I am allowed only one more question. I select something that has bewildered me ever since arriving in Constantinople.

"Armond, on more than one occasion people have referred to Dr. Demirr as a railroad doctor." The corporal nods his head in agreement. "I do not understand. The doctor does not travel on trains so why do they call him that?"

"Oh, my friend, you misunderstand its meaning. Listen carefully and learn something." I toss my buffing cloth aside and sit next to Armond as he shares something intriguing. "During the early stages of the war, all the wounded soldiers who arrived in the city were taken directly to the hospitals regardless of the severity of their injuries. It overcrowded the medical facilities so much that some soldiers died awaiting treatment. A decision was made that one of the physicians would meet the trains when they came into the station to make the determination of sending the soldiers in one of two directions- either to the hospital or to the cemetery. Dr. Demirr was chosen to make that life or death decision. And that is why, my friend, you can always tell when a military train is coming into the city with the wounded. Yes, when the railroad doctor leaves our house, the fate of many men is on the line."

I ask no further questions. My respect for Dr. Demirr increases knowing the tremendous responsibility he bears.

~~~~~~~~~~~~~~~~~~~~~~~~~~~~~~

I am working with the gardener a few days later. His attitude toward me is a reminder that Armenians are not favored in Constantinople or anywhere the Ottoman Turks are in power. Ishmail

146

considers me a nuisance. His limited knowledge of horticulture got him his current assignment and probably saved him from serving on the battlefield.

The manicured grounds are filled with a variety of blooming flowers and sculpted shrubs. Ishmail prefers to work alone and has little use for a helper who weeks earlier was trudging to a death camp in the Syrian Desert.

"Pick up those clippings and haul them to the dump pile," he yells after trimming hedges. "Get a move on it!"

It is when I am working in the yard that I notice the windows on the third floor are shuttered. All other windows on this sunny day are open allowing brightness and fresh air to flow through the house. My curiosity is aroused.

"Why are all of the windows on the third floor closed?" I ask. The gardener is not fond of conversation while we work.

"It is none of your business," he responds. "Besides, you will never have reason to be in that part of the house."

"I didn't mean any disrespect. I was just..."

"You were just poking that Armenian nose into something that should be of no interest to you. Now, get back to work!" I am disrespected in less time than it takes the gardener to put down his shears and wipe the sweat from his brow. My curiosity increases the longer we continue to work in the yard. I am determined to learn what is so special about the third floor.

Note: In 2007, the United States Congress attempts to pass Resolution 106 which basically labels as "genocide" the deaths of Armenians during the massacres around 1915 by the Turkish Ottoman Empire. Turkey organizes a massive campaign spending hundreds of thousands of dollars in its attempt to get the resolution defeated. (Wikipedia: United States Record on the Armenian Genocide)

Chapter 23

It is three weeks since my brief conversation with the gardener concerning the secrecy surrounding the top floor of Dr. Demirr's home. I stopped asking questions about it, but then Armond summons me to the laundry room early one morning.

"Nishan, you can help me take these items to the third floor," he says, stacking a pile of sheets and pillow cases onto my outstretched arms. I can barely see over the freshly laundered linens, but that is not going to prevent me from this assignment. He grabs a dust mop and some cleaning supplies. My curiosity is about to be satisfied.

I begin to show signs of fatigue partway up the steep stairs. The pieces that seemed so light and airy in the laundry room feel as though they have added weight, but it is only my imagination.

"Now you know why no one ever goes to the third floor," Armond jokes from several stairs ahead of me. "I would think a young person like you would bounce up these stairs faster than this old soldier, especially one who took a bullet in the leg." The not so subtle attempt to embarrass me works and I step up the pace. Each landing contains beautiful chandeliers glistening with dozens of finely-cut teardrop crystals that light our way. We reach a corridor at the top of the stairs. Two massive pocket doors stand between us and the accommodations on the third floor.

Armond slips a skeleton key into the lock and tells me, "I do not come here often, just enough to air out the rooms and eliminate some dust." He grasps each door and shoves them apart. Smooth rollers send the doors in opposite directions. We now have access to a large room shaded in darkness.

"Wait here until I let some light into the room," he tells me.

I stand still watching as Armond carefully makes his way across the room to where long drapes shadow each window. He pulls the golden tassels controlling each curtain. One by one, each section of the room is engulfed in sunlight. Coming into view is a display of elegance that I have never seen before. Every item and piece of furniture in this bedroom appears not to have been disturbed in a long time. An eerie stillness fills the air.

I believe our job is done after putting the linens away, but the corporal has more work to do. A light coating of dust on furniture draws his attention, so he takes a feather duster and begins the next chore. I am excused from this work and there is time for me to explore the entire third level. Armond keeps an eye on me until I begin to wander out of the master bedroom.

"Look all you want, but do not touch anything," he cautions. I nod an acknowledgement of his instructions. There are two adjoining bedrooms to explore. I peek through the doorway of each room and discover that they are also immaculate.

"Does anyone use these rooms?" I yell to Armond in the main bedroom. The simple question brings an odd response.

"No one sleeps here anymore." There is sadness in his voice, so I return to the master bedroom to speak directly with him. He is at an open window gazing out at a blue sky filled with puffy white clouds.

"I don't understand. These are wonderful bedrooms. Why would they not be used?"

"You weren't here when we suffered through those terrible days and nights," Armond tells me without turning around. The subject seems to upset the man, so it is put aside for the moment.

I return to the smaller bedroom. The pastel colors favor that of a female child. Her hairbrush and small mirror lay undisturbed on the vanity. A heart-shaped music box shows some dust, but the most telling piece in the room captures my heart. On the dresser is a framed picture featuring a family portrait of four people. I recognize only the man who stands behind a beautiful lady seated with two children. Dr. Demirr is the proud husband and father. I want to know more about this intriguing picture, but first there is another bedroom to visit.

The last room contains clues telling me that a little boy has played many make-believe battles within its walls. My eyes glance to an open toy box in a corner of room. A war scene with toy soldiers is arranged on a nearby small table. Eight tiny British soldiers in bright red tunics aim their rifles at Arabian lancers mounted on horses at full gallop. Perhaps the child was interrupted before the imagined battle was finished. I am tempted to examine the miniature soldiers more closely, but I honor my commitment to Armond. The bathroom areas are quaint but left unexplored; there are more important matters to discuss.

"Did you enjoy your little foray through the sleeping quarters?" Armond asks when I return to the master bedroom.

"I would not call it enjoyment. It was more like curiosity if you ask me."

"There is no mystery here, only sadness. They are to be respected and not questioned by one so young." He shakes a forefinger to scold me. "These rooms belong to a man who lost everything he cherished in this world." Armond's voice softens as he reflects, "There was a time when these rooms were filled with happiness. Those days are gone... gone forever."

I believe our relationship may have been damaged because of my inquisitive behavior, but I am mistaken. Armond invites me to have a seat on a large ottoman while he shares a story with me.

"It was February of 1915. Navy ships from Britain and France launched an attack on the northwest coast of Turkey in an area called the Gallipoli Peninsula. The initiative had two objectives. It was not only to secure a vital waterway to access

Russian allies but was also to allow Allied troops to attack the Ottoman capital of Constantinople. The plan ran into difficulty when Australian and New Zealand troops meet major resistance at the beaches in the region of Gallipoli and the Dardanelles. The battles raged on for months with both sides encountering heavy losses. More than 250,000 Allied troops were counted as casualties, but the Ottomans suffer just as many losses. Dr. Demirr and other physicians were ordered into the war zone to treat the wounded soldiers. He left Constantinople and his family to labor in temporary hospitals along the trench lines for two months trying to save lives. The conditions were atrocious. Medical supplies were scarce, and yet he saw to it that many who would have died without excellent treatment lived to be reunited with their loved ones. Eventually, the Allied troops evacuated, and the Ottoman Empire claims its greatest victory of the war." He continues to tell me more.

"During all this time there was little communication from Constantinople until word came that Dr. Demirr's entire family had fallen ill. Unsanitary conditions released bacteria, and typhoid spread among the population of the capital city. The doctor requested a leave of absence to return to his family. The request was denied, and he spent another month in the trenches keeping others alive while his loved one's clung to life on the third floor of this house. Dr. Demirr was finally allowed to return home, but the family had perished."

I am speechless when Armond finishes. He pauses long enough to settle his emotions. Most likely, he has shared the story before, but it remains heartbreaking.

"So, now you know the story of a man who sacrificed everything in the name of humanity. Those who fight against the Ottomans call us evil people but how can someone who lost his entire family for the sake of his fellow man be anything but a saint?" I am not the only person in the room with tears in my eyes. Armond and I share the same emotion as he ends the story. "It is as I told you. There is no mystery to the third level of this home. Dr. Demirr no longer comes here. The pain is too great. We leave it exactly as it was during the happier times out of respect for this man."

My thoughts are of Dr. Demirr when we exit the third floor. A place filled with the memories of a loving family.

Note: May 7, 1915. A German U-boat torpedoes and sinks the RMS Luistania while the British ocean liner is enroute from New York to Liverpool, England. More than 1,100 people perish, including 128 Americans. Nearly two years pass before the United States enters World War I. (Wikipedia: Lusitania)

Chapter 24

Changes are taking place in Constantinople that effect our routine within the Demirr household. Although the Ottoman Empire claims victory in the battle for control of the Gallipoli Peninsula, the loss of soldiers devastates the Turkish military. Younger recruits filter into the capital city to be given physical examinations before being sent to the battlefields.

Dr. Demirr and other staff of the hospital must now extend their duties beyond caring for the wounded. Mother and I have proven to be trusted members of the household staff. The doctor now elects to utilize us at the hospital. I find it unsettling that we are engaged in activities that benefit soldiers fighting against those who are bravely trying to save the Armenians. There is no choice; to refuse could mean the end of our protected situation living in Constantinople. Mother will assist in the examination room, and I am assigned to keep areas clean to reduce the risk of infections. This new assignment may alter our future.

Turkish recruits are seated in a hallway outside the examination room at the hospital. I am fulfilling my duties inside the same room as Mother when she calls each soldier's name to meet with the doctor. The exam usually takes only a few minutes. The criteria to qualify are greatly reduced due to the need for troops on the battlefield. The Ottomans fear that the United States of America is inching closer to entering World War I on the side of the Allies. If this happens, every Turk who can shoot a gun will be needed, regardless of their age or physical condition.

Mother's duties require providing a record of each soldier's examination results. She understands enough of the language to file an accurate report based on the findings. It is seldom that a recruit fails the physical requirements. On this day, however, there is an exception.

A soldier enters the room and pays little attention to me as I continue to use a cloth and alcohol to sterilize the medical instruments and equipment. He cordially greets my mother and Dr. Demirr initiates the examination routine.

"What is your name and age, soldier?"

"Hasan, sir. I am eighteen years old today" he answers respectfully.

"Hmm, next we will be enlisting babies to fight this war," the doctor states. Then, he notices the young man wavering back and forth.

"Soldier are you okay?"

"I feel sort of dizzy and a little sick to my stomach, sir."

"A lot of recruits get nervous before being sent to the front lines. That may be causing your problem."

"Maybe so, sir. It did somewhat upset me when my request to be exempted was denied."

"You asked to be excused from military service? That's not so unusual. Not everyone wants to die for their country." The soldier takes exception to the comment.

"I am not afraid to die, sir. I just don't believe in killing people."

"I cannot say that I disagree with you. Unfortunately, we don't have much say in the matter when it comes to world politics."

"I understand, sir, but even that will not make me kill another human being." This strong belief may get him killed once he reaches the battlefield. The examination moves to the next level.

The soldier steps forward to hand Mother his documents, but they slip from his hand and drop to the floor. He reaches for the papers and stumbles forward. She catches him in time to prevent the fall. He is in no condition to stand, so she lowers him to the floor as Dr. Demirr rushes to assist.

"It looks like we have a sick man here, Mary. You better get a pillow under his head while I see what's going on with this fellow. What did he say his name is?"

"Hasan," Mother replies as she hurries to retrieve a pillow from a nearby cot. In the seconds it takes for her to return, the man's condition takes a dramatic turn for the worse. He curls into a fetal position, moaning that the room is spinning.

The situation is traumatic. Mother comforts the soldier by holding his hand as Dr. Demirr kneels over him calling out symptoms. The cadence comes right out of a medical journal. "Rapid heartbeat... heavy perspiration... cold chills... nausea... dizziness." The doctor's professional expertise comes forth with compassion, "Hasan, we are here to help you. Try to relax while I ascertain what is causing your illness."

The soldier responds, but it comes in spurts. Every utterance is followed by a deep breath and groaning. "Yes, sir... I'm cold... please cover me."

I have never seen anything like this. Sweat is dripping from the soldier's pores, but he shivers as though he were standing stark naked in a blizzard. Dr. Demirr tells me to retrieve blankets from a storage cabinet. I immediately do as he asked and hand them to Mother. She places them on the soldier even though sweat continues to seep from his pores.

"Do you think we should get him onto the cot?" Mother asks Dr. Demirr.

"No, Mary. He is likely to eliminate the contents of his stomach or his bowels if we try to move him. It is best to let him lie here until this episode passes. Place a damp washcloth on his forehead. It may give him some relief." She follows the instructions and gets a pleasant surprise when the soldier murmurs a response.

"Thank you, Mary. *(gasp)* Sorry to be *(gasp)* so much trouble."

"It's alright, Hasan. You try to rest and let the doctor help you." She comforts him as the doctor tries to determine what is causing the illness.

"I thought at first it might be an infection, or perhaps the constriction of a blood vessel. Now, I'm not sure it's either." He initiates a series of questions to help with a diagnosis. "Hasan, do you have these dizzy spells often?"

"Just started *(gasp)* two weeks ago."

"That is good information," Dr. Demirr tells the soldier. "Have you had a fever or high temperature prior to this dizziness?"

"No, sir, *(gasp)* I don't think so."

"Just one more question and then you can rest. Okay?" Hasan attempts to shake his head, but even the slightest movement produces a groan and he remains silent. "Have you recently had an injury?" There is no response. Mother wonders if he even heard the question. Then, a faint response comes.

"Two weeks ago. *(gasp)* Did not want to say anything."

"Was the injury to your head or possibly even close to your ear?" Evidently, the doctor seems to be on to something, and the soldier's reply confirms his suspicion.

"Training drill. *(gasp)* Rifle butt hit me."

"Did the spinning and dizziness begin shortly after that?"

"Not right away. (gasp) Ringing first. *(gasp)* Dizziness that night."

"Doctor, do you think the blow to his head caused this trauma?" Mother asks.

"Yes; more precisely, a direct blow to the ear. I think Hasan has a classic case of Meniere's."

"I have never heard this," she says, while keeping her eyes trained on the ailing soldier.

"Most people haven't. There are usually no outward signs until something triggers an episode. The injury probably affected the nerves and canals in the ear that control balance. Bending over threw off his equilibrium, and that started a downward spiral within his body."

"Am I going *(gasp)* to die?"

"No, Hasan, you are not going to die. In fact, if my diagnosis is correct, you should be feeling better in a few hours."

"Is there anything we can do for him?" Mother asks.

"I am not aware of a cure for Meniere's, but it is not known to be fatal. Mary, I think you should remain close by and let him rest. This should pass with time."

Mother continues to go about her duties, but she never strays far from the room where the ill soldier lies resting on the floor. She often freshens the damp cloth that gives him relief. Her pleasant conversation lets him know she is nearby. Each time, Hasan expresses his appreciation for her attention to his welfare.

I remain close to the examination room where Mother stays with the ill soldier. There are other rooms to clean but eventually I work my way back to the room where the episode happened. Mother places a finger to her lips signaling that I should enter the room quietly. The soldier is just now opening his eyes after a lengthy rest.

"I believe someone must be feeling better!" she tells the soldier when his eyes focus on her.

"Yes, but I still feel rather weak." He tries to rise but wobbles. Mother quickly assists him into a chair. "Mary, I am sorry for the mess," he says, pointing to the disheveled sheets and soaked blankets.

"Don't worry about those things. My son will help clean that up later," she says, and nods at me standing across the room.

"This is your son?"

"Yes, Nishan is very helpful. He works at the hospital and at the doctor's home."

"It is nice that your son can be with you." Mother thinks Hasan is merely being cordial, but his remark holds more substance. "I assume you are Armenian. Not many of your people are still together because of the deportation." The misleading term is an irritation that Mother refuses to ignore.

"I think you are referring to the genocide of my people," she angrily states. She fears there will be repercussions if others learn of her comment. "I apologize. It was not good of me to speak in that manner."

The soldier's response shows maturity beyond his years. "Mary, not all Turkish people hate Armenians. I am sorry for what is happening to your people." His genuine smile lets her know everything is fine between them.

"Thank you. It is kind of you to share this with me."

"It is I who should be thanking you, Mary. I hope to repay your wonderful compassion someday." The tender moment between two people who respect one another's cultures is interrupted by the sound of footsteps.

"I see our *patient* is feeling better," Dr. Demirr calls out when entering the room.

"Yes, sir. Thank you for what you did for me."

"No thanks are necessary. I am just doing my job. The lady next to you is the one to thank. Mary stayed with you throughout the entire episode." Mother keeps her head lowered to avoid revealing the blush that shows on her cheeks. Dr. Demirr returns to the issue regarding the soldier's required examination. "There is no way I will approve you for military service. I have already informed your commanding officer that you will be recommended for a deferment."

"I don't understand, sir."

"Your medical condition makes you a detriment to your own troops," he tells the recruit. "Can you imagine our soldiers in a critical battle situation while you are undergoing a violent Meniere's episode? Why, you might change the entire course of the war!" Hasan doesn't immediately realize the humor in Dr. Demirr's exaggeration, but Mother understands and tries not to laugh out loud. She notices something about the doctor that seems to have been missing. He has a wry sense of humor that has come to the surface lately.

"You make a good point, doctor. I would not want to endanger our own men if a dizzy spell hits me."

"I cannot exempt you from public service. However, I do have the authority to assign you to a duty where your affliction may not be as much of a concern."

"That will be fine with me, sir."

"Very good. I will recommend you serve as a gendarme stationed in Constantinople. Our police in this city do not have to deal with much violent crime. They generally patrol the harbor area watching for people trying to illegally get out of the country." Mother knows the reason for such activity. Armenians and other persecuted nationalities consider the seaport a passageway to freedom. The notion is froth with danger; one slip-up brings death. We have made no attempt to escape from the city. Fear of dying is the obvious deterrent, but there is also concern for the doctor. He would be severely disciplined for his lack of oversight if two Armenians under his charge suddenly disappeared. He is the only reason we are not being held captive in a death camp. We will not jeopardize this man's safety.

"You need to be aware of certain things that may trigger another episode," the doctor instructs Hasan. "Avoid abrupt movements that can cause the fluid in your ear to shift and be careful how you bend to pick things up."

"Yes, sir. I've learned my lesson about that."

"I believe we are finished here. You can leave now if you're feeling okay." The doctor leaves the room and the soldier purposely takes extra time gathering his belongings. He again expresses appreciation to my mother, which she graciously accepts.

"You are very welcome, Hasan. I think you will be a good gendarme."

"Thank you, Mary. I consider you a friend."

Mother believes it is the last time she will see the pleasant young man, but fate has a way of changing one's life when it is least expected.

Note: "In 1933, Franz Werfel publishes *Forty Days at Musa Dagh*, a novel about the courageous but doomed resistance of Armenian villagers during the Armenian genocide. When MGM studios announce plans to make a film of the novel, the Turkish government applies pressure through the U.S. State Department and succeeds in stopping production." (Suny: History of the Armenian Genocide)

Chapter 25

"I requested that the two of you meet with me because I have something to share," Dr. Demirr says, referring to an envelope he opened minutes earlier. "You may want to sit down."

Mother and I have a seat on the comfortable couch which adorns the study. "Is something wrong, doctor?" Mother asks.

"You requested several weeks ago that I make inquiries regarding your two friends that were with you during the deportation from Amasia."

"Yes, Arixie and Yeggi. You have news about them?" We are anxious to hear about our friends, but the doctor shows little enthusiasm.

"I sent communications to Aleppo and Der ez Zor weeks ago," he says, referring to the concentration camps. "I received a reply today. There is no Arixie Enjaian or 'Yeggi' Yeghesian listed at either location. I am sorry."

Mother uses a handkerchief to dry her tears. Her words soften. "They never made it. They perished."

"Mary, those camps maintain very poor records. They are holding thousands of people." He takes her hand to give her comfort. "Your friends may very well be alive."

"Thank you for trying to find them," she says, clinging to a glimmer of hope. "Their fate has always been in the Lord's hands. Nishan and I will continue to pray every day for them."

~~~~~~~~~~~~~~~~~~~~~~~~~~~~~~~

Dr. Demirr gives Mother an assignment a few days later. She is to coordinate a special dinner to be held at the house. Leaders of the Ottoman Empire have invited dignitaries from other countries to Constantinople. Some of the invitees are not friendly with the Turkish nation. The war is not going well for the hosts. It is a final effort to dissuade the United States from committing troops to the Allied cause. This reception is disguised as a humanitarian initiative to discuss exchanging wounded prisoners of war for them to receive medical attention from doctors in their home countries. The noble idea receives little support from the Turks. The stately residence adds to the supposed theme of the event. Dr. Demirr selects my mother not only for her talent with cuisine, but also to help take her mind off the disappointing report regarding our friends from Amasia. Hopefully, focusing her attention on this assignment will give her a renewed spirit.

Note: Not all Ottomans were a threat to the Armenians. Ahmed Rize, a founder of the Young Turk movement, opposed the cruel treatment of Armenians. As a member of the Ottoman Senate, he demanded the government explain its policy toward the Armenians. He spoke out against the deportation of Armenians. (Suny: History of the Armenian Genocide)

Chapter 26

Today I travel to the market with Armond and my mother to purchase groceries and goods. We ride in a truck that will hold many items for the reception. Armond will leave us in the market district while he runs other errands. We will meet him later at a designated shop to load Mother's purchases. The event is in four days; there is much to do and little time to prepare.

"I hope everything we need is on this list," Mother exclaims as she runs her finger down a long sheet of paper listing cooking items. "I do not want to ask Armond to bring us back to the market," she tells me. "He has his own work to do getting ready for this affair."

"I really do not mind, Miss Mary," Armond says, focusing his attention on the person beside him. The distraction causes a jerk to the steering wheel, and we suddenly veer to the edge of the road. An agile pedestrian jumps out of the way in time to avoid being hit by the front fender of the truck. The man makes an obscene gesture as we speed past him. Armond makes light of the near miss and yells out the window. "Hey, you crazy person! Watch where you walk or next time Armond will not be so nice to miss you!" I snicker, but my mother is not as amused.

"Armond, it's nice of you to transport us whenever we need to go somewhere, but if you continue to drive in this manner, our destination may be the graveyard."

"Miss Mary, you are such a funny lady. I would never do anything to hurt you or Nishan. He is my favorite Armenian boy!" We laugh, but then I think about what he said. Our cultures are different and always will be.

He leaves us in a section of the city where there are many stores and an abundance of street vendors. The open-air pavilions feature fresh fruits and vegetables which will be selected for serving at the reception. Lamb meat will be chosen for the kebabs. The makings for halva, simit, rice with chick peas, baklava, and boza are just a few of the items on her shopping list. The menu is predominately Turkish, but Mother will look for some foods that may be favored by the American guests. She has learned that apple pie is a favorite dessert in the United States, and considerable effort will be put forth in the kitchen paring apples and baking crusts. The truck will be filled by the time she finishes shopping. My job is simple on this day. I am to carry the purchases to a location where they will be held awaiting Armond's arrival with the truck.

Two hours later, I am exhausted from several trips back and forth to the spot where we will meet Armond. My work is finished, and I am free to do as I please while Mother visits a few more places for small items. She gives me money to purchase something to eat. The two lira mean I can have a very good meal.

"Do not stray too far from where we are to meet the truck," she cautions. "The streets are dangerous, especially for us." I understand her message and find a comfortable place to rest beneath olive trees in a park close to the shopping area.

Two teenage boys arrive close by and scratch a large circle on a patch of dirt. I am curious about what they are up to. They reach into their pockets and drop a handful of glass balls in the middle of the circle. I have not played with marbles since my days in Amasia, but the game continues to fascinate me. Seeing the shiny spheres brings back fond memories of the fun times spent with Zaven and Aram. I continue to get excited as I watch the two young strangers prepare for the game excites me.

"Hey, do you want to play the game with us?" one of the boys asks.

"Yes, I would like to, but I have no marbles."

"That's okay; you can use some of ours," the fellow responds and waves for me to join the two of them. I hurry to the circle of dirt where we make introductions.

"I am Omer, and my friend is Yusuf. We usually play card games in the park. Our favorite game is Skambil because it only takes one deck of cards, but today we shoot marbles."

"I am Nishan. Thank you for letting me play." The partners give a suspicious look to one another when they hear my name. I wonder if they might be opportunists who view an Armenian boy as their prey.

Omer hands me several marbles that are of low-quality and chipped. I notice he and his friend are using balls that are perfectly round. "Sorry, those are the only extra ones we have for you," Omer says when he sees me examining the flaws in each ball. I am anxious to play, so I overlook the attempt to slant the game in their favor.

I squat to the ground to examine the circled arena. It is on a slope and my two opponents are kneeling on the upper rim of the circle. They have the advantage of shooting downward so that their marbles will gain momentum. Chipped marbles and having to shoot uphill puts me at a severe disadvantage. I will not make this an issue. After all, it's only a game.

The three of us choose what appears to be our best marble. I have no large or fancy ones to use as the taw, so I pick one with the least amount of damage. The rest go in the middle of the circle. The game is about to start when an awkward question arises.

"Do you have money?" Yusuf asks me.

"Yes, for my lunch," I respond.

"Well, we like to play for money. You cannot play if you don't put up some money. It's the rules," he tells me and tosses a small pouch in my direction. I hesitate, so he tempts me further. "What are you afraid of? If you win, you will have even more money." I should know better, but the challenge is too great. I pull one coin from my pocket and place it inside the pouch.

"Aren't you two going to put your lira in it, too?" I ask, after tossing the small piece of leather containing my coin back to Yusuf.

"No, it is not necessary," Omer answers. "We will drop our coins in if we lose." I indicate my discomfort with the arrangement and trigger a harsh reaction. "If you don't like it, you can just give back the marbles and leave! It is just like an Armenian to not trust us!" My honor is being challenged, so I will play the game on their terms.

The first round of the game begins. I need to quickly become accustomed to my flawed marbles. Omer shoots his taw and breaks the cluster of marbles. They scatter throughout the circle, but none leave the ring. Yusuf takes the next shot and manages to knock two balls outside the circle. He brags that it was a great shot, but I know it is not exceptional since they were resting against each other when the taw made contact. Yusuf is entitled to another shot which he misses. It is my turn. I lean forward, being careful to not have my fingers over the boundary line. The chipped marble feels awkward, but I shoot it anyway. It takes a crooked course, hits nothing solid, and comes to a dead stop in the dirt. This contest is going to be a greater challenge than I imagined. Twenty minutes later, we are in the third round and I am fortunate to still be in the game. It has been difficult having to overcome the poor quality of my marbles and shoot on uneven terrain. The game remains even only because I have eliminated enough of Omer and Yusuf's marbles. My use of a new taw comes from one of the captured marbles. The game takes a new twist.

"Look at you!" Omer calls out to me. "You are shooting very well. Perhaps we should make the wager more interesting."

"What do you mean by more interesting?" I ask. Nearly half an hour has been spent shooting partially-round glass balls on an unlevel circle, and I'm still in the game. How much more interesting can it get? The answer comes quickly.

"If you will wager another coin, Yusuf and I will double your bet."

"You mean the two of you will each put up two more to my one?"

"That is exactly what we intend to do!" An excited Yusuf joins in the conversation. "I will prove that it will be fair for you. Just watch me." He pulls six coins from his pocket and drops them inside the pouch. "That's two from us on the first bet, and another four coins for the new challenge."

I have never wagered money, but this is an opportunity to triple the amount Mother gave me. The game continues against two strangers who appear to be no better than me.

The challenge becomes more intense after the restart. The two boys are remarkably improved this session. Their shots are crisper and right on target. I believe they may have been intentionally playing beneath their skill level during the earlier rounds. The final game arrives. It is so close that any one of us can be the winner. We each have a last shot at four remaining marbles.

Yusuf has the first shot and elects to go after a marble that is close to the boundary line. It is not much of a challenge. He easily knocks it outside the circle. Omer is next to shoot. He takes his time to consider the strategy of his shot. This game will be over if he can capture at least two of the remaining marbles. I would be left with only a single target. It will not be enough to salvage my two liras. I watch as he takes aim at two marbles that are close to each other. If his shot strikes between them with enough impact, both targets could make it outside the circle. Omer will win the game and I will lose my two coins. He makes a good shot. Both balls roll toward the perimeter of the ring. One makes its way outside the circle, but the second marble rolls to a stop just short of the line. I am relieved but still must make a difficult shot to even tie the game. I now learn that the standard rules of the game have changed.

"You have to get both marbles out with one shot or else you're a loser. That's the rules," Omer shouts to me from the other side of the circle. He and Yusuf are looking very confident that they will be leaving the park with additional money.

"You never said anything about this rule before we started." My protest is anticipated and brings forth a lecture.

"It has always been the rule," Yusuf tells me. "You cannot tie the game on the last shot. Knock out the two remaining marbles or you lose."

I doubt this rule ever existed until a few moments ago, and it poses a predicament. The two teenagers are holding my money, and I will likely lose if we get into a tussle. Nevertheless, I am not going to stand by and let them cheat me.

I take some time to examine my taw for any flaws that might alter the shot. It gives me an opportunity to capture a fond memory. My friend, Zaven, is still with me in spirit: *"First, a bit of spit to eliminate any dirt, a vigorous rub to make it shine, and then a kiss for good luck. That is how you win the game, Nishan!"*

The two friends make fun of me for delaying the game. They continue to taunt and laugh as I follow the superstitious ritual acquired from my friend in Amasia. I am ready to end the game.

I ease onto my belly to study the positioning of the remaining marbles. The only shot available is to hit one marble hard enough to cause a ricochet that will send both remaining balls out of the ring. The shot is more difficult than Omer's previous attempt. The marbles he hit were almost touching; my two are not even close to each other. The odds of accomplishing this are stacked against me.

I clutch the taw in my palm and pucker my lips. Then I launch a wad of spittle onto the marble. After a few moments of buffing, I give the shiny ball a kiss for good luck. It is now ready for action. The taw is cradled with my forefinger and firmly braced from behind with my thumb. There is no need for further preparation. A powerful flick of my thumb sends the glass ball in motion. It takes flight and splatters dirt when it hits the ground moving rapidly toward a target. It hits the first marble hard enough to shatter glass, but the ball remains intact and ricochets in the direction of the second marble. In a split second, the two marbles bang together and spin in opposite directions. I hold my breath and stare as each one passes over the crude line drawn in the dirt.

"I did it! I made the shot!" A sense of joy fills my body as I leap to my feet and cheer out loud. Passersby turn their heads to see what is causing so much excitement. My two opponents are standing with their jaws hanging open.

"You cheated," Omer yells. "Nobody can make a marble jump out their hand that way and knock two balls out of the ring." Yusuf remains silent and continues to gaze at the empty ring, amazed at what he just witnessed.

"There was no cheating. It was a legal shot. Now, may I have the money which was won in a fair match?" I expect Omer to hand over my two coins and the other six. Instead, he turns his attention to Yusuf.

"The Armenian thinks we are foolish enough to give this to him," he says while repeatedly tossing the money pouch into the air. The two friends break into a degrading laugh, and I realize they have duped me. Without warning, the boys take off running; Yusuf has all the marbles and Omer clutches the pouch filled with the wagered money. I spot a gendarme entering the park and run to him to report the theft. The two scoundrels who lack principles are still in sight.

"There they are! You can still catch them if you hurry."

The gendarme seems more interested in lecturing me than enforcing the law. He takes his time studying my features. I suspect he is trying to see if I am Turkish or Armenian. Once his curiosity is satisfied, he speaks to me in a stern voice. "Perhaps you should not make this an issue."

"Sir, it is an issue. They stole my money!"

The man shows no interest, and his response explains why. "I think it is for your own good to forget this incident. Those two will likely claim that you are a lying Armenian."

"I am not lying, and what difference does it matter whether I'm Armenian, Greek, Turkish or any other nationality? They stole from me and should be punished!" My plea falls on deaf ears. The man's discrimination because of who I am hurts much more than the crime of stealing.

~~~~~~~~~~~~~~~~~~~~~~~~~~~

I meet Armond at the predetermined location. The truck is already loaded with goods from the market and we await my mother's arrival. I decide to share the earlier bad experience with Armond.

"It's too bad that happened, but you should have realized they never intended for you to leave with any money."

"I know that now. It was foolish of me to risk the liras Mother entrusted to me."

"This should be a good lesson to be more careful around strangers who pretend to be friends." My disappointment clearly shows. Armond attempts to cheer me up. "Nishan, if it only cost you two coins that is a very inexpensive education!" He laughs and gives me a friendly slap on the back.

"Please don't tell my mother. It will disappoint her."

"That will be something between you and Miss Mary, my impulsive friend. It's your decision." She approaches and we end the conversation.

"Paree!" (Greetings!) Have you two been waiting very long?" The cheerful hello means she is feeling very good about her trip to the market. She has forgotten that we agreed to use our native language only when it is just the two of us.

"I am finished loading your purchases, Miss Mary," Armond says while placing the packages she carries into the truck.

We are returning to the house when the dreaded question surfaces. "Nishan, did you have enough time to go for lunch?" Mother is so happy today. It would be a shame for me to spoil the occasion because of my stupidity in the park. Thankfully, she does not inquire about what I ate, how much it cost, or even where I had lunch. I am ashamed by my response, even though it is not an actual lie.

"Yes, Mother, I had plenty of time."

Note: Armenians are known for talent in the preparation of foods. Examples: Shish Kebab (shewered lamb with vegetables), Pasterma (dried spiced beef), Pilaf (cooked rice, vermicelli, and noodles), Katah (coffee cake), Choereg (breaded sweet bread, Paklava (sweet, layered pastry), Beoreg (turnover with cheese filling), Dolma (wrapped grape leaves with meat, rice, etc.) (AGBU: Treasured Armenian Recipes)

Chapter 27

Several additional workers are in the kitchen early on the morning of the reception. Mother lets me sleep later than usual after working into the evening helping with the preparations. Footsteps in the adjoining room awaken me. I rise to check out who has entered our quarters.

"Ishmail, I did not hear you knock. Is there something you need?" The gardener standing at a bedroom dresser abruptly turns around and gives a nervous reply.

"Uh, yes, there you are." He pauses to gather his thoughts before explaining his presence. "I wanted to make sure you knew not to report for work in the yard. Your assignment is in the kitchen today."

"Ishmail, I already know it. You told me about it two days ago."

"Oh, yes, I remember that now," he says nervously. "I am sorry to disturb you." He turns to leave, and I notice a small bag in his hand. Evidently, he had it when entering the room.

"Is that something for my mother?" I ask, pointing to the pouch that appears to be empty.

"No. I use this to hold my keys. Now, go back to sleep." He quickly exits the room. I get dressed and go to the kitchen to report this strange encounter.

Mother is concerned when I tell her about the gardener entering our quarters. She wants to think it over before speaking with Dr. Demirr. Right now, preparation for tonight's activity is the priority.

"This food looks and smells wonderful, but I think you left some of it on you," I tell Mother while she uses a towel to wipe smears of flour from her cheeks.

"Yes, now that the Young Turk regime is running the government, they will spare no expense on this night." The array of ethnic foods is impressive, especially a highly seasoned meat that fills the entire kitchen with the smell of peppered spice.

"Mother, are you really thinking about serving basterma tonight?"

"Yes, but not as part of the main meal. It is a side dish intended for the Ottomans. I don't think the guests from other countries should have it tonight. I added some extra seasonings," she informs me. "Would you like to try some now?"

"I don't think my stomach can handle it so early in the morning."

"My son, you are wise beyond your years," Mother says with a devious grin. When she turns to check on food baking in the oven, I sneak a crescent cookie from a serving tray. Surely one missing treat filled with raisins and nuts will not be missed at tonight's reception. Mother is not fooled. A keen eye catches the theft, and my 'punishment' is a hug and a kiss. "I always bake extras just for you." She

181

hands me a second cookie before getting back to work.

"Do you think the basterma will be too spicy for their stomachs?" I ask as she pulls a tray loaded with braided choreg from the oven. After setting the tray down, she rests both hands on her hips and gives me a lecture.

"The Turks have cut off the heads of our men and slaughtered our pregnant women. I think their stomachs can handle the spiced meat!" I have learned my lesson and apologize. She takes a moment to settle her emotions. "I'm sorry to take my feelings about the Ottoman leaders out on you. I will feel better once we finish trying to help them make a good impression to other countries."

I understand the frustration and leave the topic. A compliment about her fine cooking might yield another cookie.

Note: By the end of World War I, 90% of the Ottoman Armenians were gone, killed, deported to the deserts of Syria, or refugees in the Caucasus or Middle East. (Suny: History of the Armenian Genocide)

Chapter 28

Dr. Demirr and Ottoman government officials welcome guests as they enter the dining hall. We peek from the kitchen doorway as the diplomats are seated at circular dinner tables. My mother points to the United States Ambassador assigned to the embassy in Constantinople. He is a distinguished-looking gentleman wearing a tailored business suit.

"That is Henry Morgenthau. He is a good man trying to persuade the Turks to stop killing our people," she whispers. I keep my eyes on the man from America as he takes a seat at the main table. Dr. Demirr and the Turkish Minister of War are seated next to him. Mother's hand suddenly grasps my shoulder. A frightened look comes over her as she stares at another person entering the room. There is no mistaking the jagged scar sliced into the man's face by my father's blade. Why is Sgt. Asid here?

Dinner begins following welcoming remarks related to the purpose of the meeting. Mother and her assistants bring in trays laden with dinner plates filled with splendid food. I follow with a pitcher of water to fill glasses. Seeing so many important people has me wondering why there are no military guards accompanying them.

"There are armed escorts from each country stationed outside the building. Tonight, the gendarmes stand guard in the dining hall," one of the temporary servants tells me.

Dinner goes well and there is plenty of casual conversation. The basterma, eaten mostly by Turkish guests, has the anticipated effect. Those who sampled it are taking in a lot of liquid. I do my job and repeatedly return to the kitchen to refill the water pitcher. It is not difficult work, but danger is near. Each time I enter the dining area a set of eyes follows me.

The time comes when people seated with Sgt. Asid require refills. I nervously approach with my head down to avoid eye contact. The sergeant continues to converse with other guests. He seems to pay little attention to the person filling his glass. I turn to leave, but he grabs my arm and pulls me close to him. Each stitch that pieced his pockmarked face back together is clearly visible. I am trapped and attempting to break his grip will disrupt the meeting. An outburst of laughter coming from across the room captures the attention of those sitting at this table. They are not aware of my predicament as my tormentor pulls me closer.

He leans to my ear and whispers with a menacing growl, "I will deal with you and your mother later."

The ruthless man is filled with hatred toward us. I cannot imagine what he is doing in Constantinople. I inform my mother of his presence, and she warns that we must be careful not to cross his path again. The people helping with the dinner are given specific instructions which allow us to avoid reentering the dining area. Our service the rest of the evening will be in the kitchen where we can observe the proceedings without being noticed.

The business portion of the meeting begins. A few participants give short presentations. However, it is when Dr. Demirr stands to address the group that those in attendance pay close attention to an impassioned plea:

"The wounded soldiers being held captive in foreign lands no longer represent a threat to anyone. Many are permanently disabled. They will never fight again. Yes, they receive medical attention from their captors. Nevertheless, there is no substitute for being close to loved ones.

If we disregard nationality, country, or political alignment, we are simply left with damaged humans who believe they fought for a noble cause. I come before you not as a military officer, but as a physician sworn to give aid to all who suffer. I believe my medical colleagues concur.

I ask you to unite in support of a proposal that will release soldiers who are so incapacitated they are no longer capable of military service.

Yes, this is a bold initiative. It calls for each of us to search our hearts and act in the name of humanity."

There is lengthy applause following the speech. I wonder if the enthusiasm is in support of the suggested proposal, or merely a professional courtesy afforded to the pleasant doctor.

It is during the closing minutes when the Ottoman Minister of War seizes this occasion to make a political statement. The message is in not linked to the purpose of the meeting. His conversation with the American ambassador throughout the evening has centered on a sensitive topic. He now shares it with everyone attending the meeting.

"I wish to make a few remarks regarding a matter put before me by the United States Ambassador. He and I have conversed many times regarding what has become known as the Armenian question. Perhaps my statement will put this issue to rest once and for all." The pompous man tries to be diplomatic, but he lacks the talent of a spokesperson for an entire country. "Our esteemed guest, Mr. Henry Morgenthau, seems to have a rather misguided sympathy for the people of Armenia; thus, I am moved to share with tonight's audience the Ottoman Empire's position regarding our dealings with the Armenians."

"Mother, what's going on out there?" She turns away from the kitchen door that is slightly open.

"Quiet, Nishan. I will tell you later. Whatever it is, I am sure he is up to no good." She places a finger to her lips to emphasize the need for silence. The Turkish leader continues to speak.

"I informed Mr. Ambassador that the Armenians had fair warning that if they caused trouble, there would be dire consequences. They started a revolution intended to overthrow our government. We have been quite tolerant of their actions. The deportation from their villages has been done for their own protection."

Mother is incensed by what she hears. "Lies, nothing but lies," she tells me. "The truth must be known." She finds a pencil and notepad in a kitchen drawer and hurriedly writes a note:

Mr. Ambassador,
Envar Pasha lies. My son and I were forced from our villiage in Amasia. We joined thousands of Armenians walking for days toward the prisoner camps.

Many who did not die from lack of food and water were slaughtered for no good reason. Please help the Armenians. My name is Mary Nighosian.

"Mother, what are you doing?"

"You stay in the kitchen. I am going to get this note to the Ambassador from the United States."

"It's too dangerous. Please do not go." My cries are of no use. She is determined to set the record straight, and the American dignitary may be her only opportunity. She takes my hand and tells me how much I am loved. Her lips softly touch my cheek. I worry this night may separate us forever, but it's too late for another appeal. She is out the door carrying a pitcher of water to disguise her real purpose.

I can do no more than watch from the safety of the kitchen. She briskly makes her way around tables filled with officials from various countries. There are stops occasionally to fill a glass to avoid drawing too much attention. Now, when only a few feet from the Ambassador, a gendarme stationed nearby causes her to hesitate. I pray she will return to the kitchen. The folded piece of paper is small but not completely concealed. Mother purposely avoided placing it in the apron pocket to casually pass it to the Ambassador. The gendarme is pointing at the hand containing the note. She has no choice but to surrender the fateful message.

The gendarme is being discrete so as not to cause an interruption to the important meeting. He asks my mother to step aside to inspect the contents of the note. The dinner guests pay little attention and continue to chat with one another. One individual, however, is carefully watching the situation play out. Dr. Demirr's curiosity is triggered after seeing Mother return to the dining hall so soon after the water glasses were just filled. He steps away from the table.

"Excuse me, officer. May I be of assistance?" He keeps his voice down hoping the conversation will remain private. The security guard is respectful and speaks in a similar manner.

"Sir, I saw this lady concealing something and decided to check it out." Dr. Demirr shifts his attention. The frightened look in my mother's eyes tells him something is amiss. His trusted housekeeper is fearful of the note falling into the wrong hands. Dr. Demirr must act fast before the message conveyed in the note is revealed.

"Officer, I understand and commend you for doing your duty." The flattery works, and the man's stern look turns to a smile of appreciation. Dr. Demirr continues, "The paper that you hold is a communication for me. I asked Mary to deliver it as soon as it arrived. She has done just as I instructed." Mother is bewildered by the ruse, but gladly plays along. The doctor shakes the man's hand and the situation appears to be resolved. "Now, officer, if you don't mind, I will take the note. Thank you for your diligent work."

"Yes sir, Dr. Demirr." He hands over the folded slip of paper. Before returning to his assigned post, the polite gendarme gives an apology to my mother. Then she turns her attention to a suggestion coming from a trusted source.

"Mary, I think you should fill more glasses and return to the kitchen." Dr. Demirr appears anxious that the audience's attention may be shifting away from the podium speaker. Mother complies, knowing that the doctor has once again defused a tense situation.

The American ambassador's glass is almost empty. She makes her way to his side with only the intention of pouring water. She tilts the pitcher and a voice surprises her.

"I hope we have not caused the servers too much trouble this evening," Ambassador Morgenthau tells her.

"No sir, no trouble at all. I enjoy working for the doctor."

"Yes, he appears to be a pleasant fellow. May I ask your name?

"I am Mary. And, yes, Dr. Demirr is a nice man."

"That is good to know, Mary. Heaven only knows we need more people like him, especially during these troubled times. How long have you been with the doctor?" Mother worries about spending so much time just to fill a glass of water, but the gentleman is engaging.

"Almost a year, sir. He gave my son and me shelter when we were deported." She lowers her head, embarrassed by the admission.

"Deported, you say?" The ambassador is familiar with the term.

"Yes, I am Armenian."

For the moment, Ambassador Morgenthau says nothing. He places a hand to his forehead and rubs his brow. The Armenian issue is something that has challenged him since being assigned to the embassy in Constantinople. Three years have passed, and he has yet to convince the Ottomans to acknowledge their role in the annihilation of the Armenians. The matter weighs heavily on his conscience.

Mother grows anxious of her time spent with the thoughtful gentleman. People will become curious if she stays any longer. When she starts to leave, his goodbye indicates he understands the plight of our people. "Mary, I pray the Lord will be with you and all Armenians."

The meeting is almost finished when the Ottoman Minister of War makes an announcement. He requests that Sgt. Asid stand to be acknowledged. Many battles have taken a toll on the hostile man. He uses a walking cane to steady his balance.

"I wish to introduce Sgt. Asid, a brave soldier of the Ottoman Empire. He is recovering from a battlefield wound. The sergeant recently accepted a position as an inspector with the Constantinople gendarmes. I am convinced that he will maintain a firm hand on the security of our city." There is subdued applause. The guests are either not impressed by the appointment of the soldier who has earned his share of negative criticism for barbarism during military engagements, or perhaps the audience is just weary from an evening of speeches. In either case, the meeting adjourns leaving two people in the kitchen in disbelief.

"Do you think there will be trouble because of tonight, Mother?" She has been silent for some time following the failed attempt to deliver the note.

"I'm not sure what will happen, Nishan. The doctor is a good man and loyal to his country. We cannot expect him to turn his back on his own people just for our sake."

"What about Sgt. Asid? He had a look of hate in his eyes when he grabbed me."

"My son, only God knows the answer to your questions. Say your prayers tonight."

~~~~~~~~~~~~~~~~~~~~~~~~~~~~

A soft knock comes at our door after I have gone to bed. Mother has stayed up to read her Bible. I slip out of my bed and quietly crack open my bedroom door, being curious as to who is paying a visit so late in the evening. Mother fastens the clasp on her robe and opens the door after recognizing a voice in the hallway.

"Mary, I apologize for disturbing you at this hour. I hope you were still awake." The doctor's voice sounds weary. I peek through the crack of my bedroom door to see that he still has on his formal attire from the meeting although the bowtie is loosened.

"Do you wish to come in, sir?"

"No, it's not necessary. I don't want to awaken your son." He reaches into the breast pocket of his suit jacket and hands her a slip of paper. "I am returning this to you. We are the only ones who know what is written on this piece of paper."

"I am not sure that I understand."

"I have given this matter considerable thought since the guests left." He clicks open his pocket watch to be more specific. "Well, actually, it has been almost two hours of contemplation in the study," he says with a weary sigh. "I understand your motivation in attempting to contact the American ambassador. Unfortunately, I am returning the note to you. We must both do what our hearts tell us is right."

Mother was afraid he would turn the note over to the authorities. Concealing it could be construed as an act of treason on his part. He is now apologizing for not allowing her to pass it to the intended party. Her response eases his anguish.

"Of course, I understand. You are most kind to do this."

It is a tender moment. Two people on opposite sides of the war share respect for each other. In another time, another place, they might be drawn even closer together. For now, they remain just friends.

Note: The art of winemaking has existed in Armenia from time immemorial. Noah is purported to have cultivated the first grape vines in the foothills of Mount Ararat after the Great Flood. (Rem Ananikyan: Yerevan)

Chapter 29

It is almost noon, so I head down the hallway toward the front door. This is the regular time that Kerim, the *postaci*, delivers the daily mail. He usually just slips it through the slot in the door, but today is different. I can see him on the front steps awaiting my arrival to answer his knock on the door. I open it and give a friendly smile to the young man who has always offered a pleasant handshake whenever we meet one another. He seems to be one of the Turkish people who harbor no hatred toward the Armenians.

"Hello, Nishan. I was hoping you would be the one to come for the mail."

"Yes, Kerim, is there something I can do for you?"

"Not really. It is more a question of what I may do for you and your mother." The words seem mysterious, and he proceeds to tell about something he encountered while delivering the mail to gendarme headquarters earlier this morning. "After I made my mail delivery, I decided to visit the washroom, which is down a hallway close to Inspector Asid's office. I noticed his door was partially open and I could hear him speaking to someone. The two men could not see me, but I clearly saw who was with the inspector. It was Dr. Demirr's gardener, Ishmail." He pauses to reconsider whether to share the information.

"Yes, Kerim, go on. I want to know what you overheard."

"You must promise not to tell anyone that I am the person who gave you this information. It would be very bad for me if the inspector ever found out."

"Yes, I promise. No one will know that it was you, but I still have no idea what you are talking about. Please continue."

"Here it is," Kerim says, while nervously looking over his shoulder to make sure no one on the street is watching. He then shares what he heard between Inspector Asid and Ishmail. His recall is so vivid, I can envision the vile conversation play out in my mind:

"I tell you, Asid, the Armenian woman is constantly stealing from Dr. Demirr," a skittish Ishmail says while seated in the inspector's office early in the morning. "I have personally witnessed it for quite some time with my own eyes."

"I would have very little to do with your report of petty crime, but the female you accuse is of great interest to me. Why have you not come forth with this information sooner?"

"I did not realize it was so extensive until recently. Just yesterday pieces of jewelry came up missing. Perhaps a search of her living quarters will reveal where it is stashed."

"Is there any other reason for your recent sense of civic responsibility?" Asid asks.

"Well, yes. I am no longer employed by Dr. Demirr. I leave today and wish to set the record straight before I depart."

"Tell me why you are parting company with the doctor. I am told he is very gracious with the people who work around him."

"Yes, that is true. Perhaps we should just call it a difference of opinion."

"That's really doesn't answer the question. You need to do better than that if you expect me to place any validity to your story."

"Alright, if you must know, Dr. Demirr is a fine physician but, he knows very little about growing vegetables and nurturing flowers. In fact, I believe he knows very little about growing anything."

"And, you are an expert on horticulture?"

"Well, maybe not an expert, but I do know the difference between roses and zinnias," he responds. The inspector does not look convinced the gardener is telling the truth, but it matters little to him.

"I readily admit that my knowledge of flowers is limited, but I believe there is more to this story than you are telling."

"Inspector, why would you think that?"

"Demirr and I may have philosophical differences, but he is a worldly person. I venture to say he knows more about horticulture than most of Constantinople. A wise man does not always share just how smart he is." Asid pauses and then continues. "Let's get down to business. If what you tell me is the truth, my interest is seeing that the Armenian woman is severely punished."

"Of course, it's the truth. I would bet my life on it!" Ishmail shouts. Inspector Asid's confident look indicates the gardener may have gone too far with that assurance.

"That is good to know, my sneaky friend. I will keep it in mind during my visit with the doctor later today."

"I don't get your meaning. Exactly what will you keep in mind?"

"I am merely agreeing with you," Asid says. He walks around the desk and presses a finger squarely into Ishmail's chest. "You have staked your measly life on this matter. If my investigation reveals that you have lied to a gendarme inspector of the Ottoman Empire, you will pay the ultimate price." Ishmail looks pale but gets little sympathy.

Kerim ends his tale and I thank him for confiding in me. He departs only after requesting that I not reveal the source of my new information. Some things are now clearer to me. I know the reason for Ishmail's visit to our living quarters was to plant items that would place suspicion on my mother as stealing from Dr. Demirr. More importantly, I realize there is impending danger coming in the days ahead.

Note: On November 11, 1918, Germany signs an armistice with the Allies. This becomes the official date for the end of

World War I. The fate of Armenia is still unknown. (Wikipedia: Timeline of World War I)

Chapter 30

I am busy dusting furniture in a room next to the study when I hear Dr. Demirr greet someone at the front door. I glance down the hallway to see who has arrived and shudder at the sight of my worst enemy. What business could Asid possibly have with the doctor?

I press my body behind the door leading into the room I have been cleaning as the two men pass by on their way to the study. I think whatever has brought Asid into this residence cannot be good for us. The two men enter the study, leaving the door slightly ajar. My curiosity is peaked as I move dangerously close to watch and listen.

"I have come here on a matter of great importance," the inspector says while seated across the desk from Dr. Demirr.

"Asid, I can't imagine what we could possibly have to discuss." His dislike for the retired soldier is evident. Asid's reputation for killing helpless women and children is known throughout the Ottoman Empire.

"I have learned from a somewhat reliable source that the Armenian woman, Mary Nighosian, has been stealing from you. If this is true, I intend to arrest her and see that she is duly punished." He adds to the accusation. "I believe the boy is likely involved too. Asid's mention of me is frightening.

"May I inquire as to the name of this reliable source?" the doctor inquires.

"Umm, I prefer to have the name remain confidential for the time being," the inspector answers with a strained smile. "Surely you understand that an ongoing investigation must be handled with the utmost discretion." Asid has been on the job less than a week. His language sounds like it comes directly from a gendarme training manual. Dr. Demirr's look tells me he is not impressed.

"That is fine with me if you wish to play games; I will play along just to humor you." The doctor places a finger to his temple and looks to the ceiling as though he is in deep thought. "Let me think about this for a moment." Suddenly, he pretends to capture an idea. "Yes, of course! Your somewhat reliable source is Ishmail, the former gardener whom I dismissed last evening." Asid leans back in his chair, surprised the snitch's name came so easily. I, too, am surprised. Evidently Dr. Demirr does not intend to make an announcement that Ishmail is no longer on the staff. Perhaps he believes it is a private matter and allows Ishmail to remain on cordial terms with the rest of us.

"Congratulations, perhaps we should enlist your services with our investigations, Doctor."

"No, thank you. I prefer to choose the company I keep." The obvious insult does not sit well with the inspector.

"Yes, I understand completely. And, I believe if a certain lieutenant in the Ottoman Empire were to have spent even one day fighting on the front lines, we might not be having this conversation." He follows with a statement that cannot be misconstrued. "After all, some useless officers have been known to be executed by their own men." A soldier could be court-martialed for the veiled threat, but Asid is no longer in the military. Dr. Demirr keeps a calm demeanor throughout the exchange. There are more important matters to address.

"I assume we are finished firing innuendos, so why don't we get down to business? What is it you want to accomplish today?

"I wish to confront the woman regarding the theft of your valuables."

"Okay, I'm comfortable having you speak to Mary, but first you need to know something." Asid listens while the doctor shares something only he and Armond know. "Mary is no thief. If anyone is to be arrested, it should be Ishmail. He has stolen from me for the past two years."

I am pleased that the doctor is defending my mother, and I still suspect the reason Ishmail came to our room the other night was to shift the blame for the thefts onto my mother.

"You knew the man was stealing from you, and yet you kept him employed? That does not seem very smart to me."

"You do not know the whole story. Perhaps it will help if I fill you in."

"Yes, I love nothing more than to hear how an intelligent person such as you can be fooled by his gardener."

"Correction, that would be my former gardener. Ishmail is packing and will soon be out of here."

"Okay, are you going to tell me the story or not?" The inspector grows anxious wondering what all of this has to do with his investigation. Before continuing, Dr. Demirr takes time to gaze at a portrait of his father displayed over the fireplace. The inspector grows impatient. "The story, please!"

"Oh, sorry, my thoughts must have drifted for a few moments. Let's see, where shall I begin?" He then proceeds to explain that Ishmail's father worked for the Demirr family for thirty-nine years. He worked hard and was quite trustworthy; however, he came to realize that his son was lazy and likely not to go far in life. As the man approached the end of his life, Dr. Demirr's father promised to give Ishmail employment until he reached his thirtieth birthday. "You see, Inspector, it is a matter of principle. My father passed away two years ago. I honor him by fulfilling the promise. Ishmail turned thirty at midnight. His time with this household has expired."

"Alright, I can understand keeping someone on the staff because of your father's promise, but it doesn't answer why you let him continue taking your valuables. That is foolish if you ask me."

"Yes, I am sure there are many others who will agree with you. It has been two years and the only items to have disappeared are trinkets, some custom jewelry, a variety of foods, and some very cheap wine."

"How do you know that is all he has taken?"

"Obviously, I cannot be positive, but most of my wealth is either in a vault or secured elsewhere. Nothing that I treasure is missing." Inspector Asid questions the validity of the story, but the doctor is prepared to back it up. "Armond will confirm everything I have told you."

"Cpl. Armond is aware of this entire story?"

"Yes, and by the way, it is now Sgt. Armond. He recently received a promotion in rank. I am sorry to say that he also will be leaving me. It is his decision."

"He has been with you many years. What are his plans?"

"Armond is a career soldier. He would tell you that it is his destiny to live or die as a soldier. Such a romantic," the doctor says with an affectionate smile. "He leaves today."

My concentration is interrupted by the sound of footsteps coming down the stairs. I will be discovered eavesdropping in mere seconds, so I quickly return to the adjacent room and watch Armond approach the study. He gives a polite knock on the door and enters. When it appears safe, I return to my listening spot.

"Excuse me, Dr. Demirr. I was not aware you had company." Armond recognizes the visitor and avoids shaking his hand. Asid has never been on friendly terms with the trusted military aide. "I merely wish to tell you goodbye unless there is anything else you wish for me to do for you." Dr. Demirr is happy to see the man who protected him on many dangerous assignments.

"I hoped you would stop by before starting your new adventure, Armond." He looks over the congenial soldier's attire. "You certainly look snappy in that new uniform, Sergeant. The ladies will be swooning over you."

"Oh, Doctor, you make fun of me, but that is why I like you so much. It was kind of you to make the recommendation. I will do my best to be a good sergeant."

"I have no doubt that your men will respect you, Armond. That is important, especially in battle." Asid nervously fidgets in his chair. The doctor's comment seems to address qualities lacking in the man who received little respect from his own troops during his military years. "Inspector Asid has come today with an accusation that Mary has stolen from the household."

"Miss Mary stealing? No, sir, I do not believe she would steal from anyone, especially you."

"I agree; however, the inspector says he has a witness. Do you have any idea who that might be?" Armond scratches his beard while considering the question. He is in no hurry to answer, although he has known the identity of the thief for years. The more the inspector shuffles in his chair, the longer

Armond drags on the suspense. Finally, the answer comes out.

"It is that scoundrel Ishmail. I have watched him pilfer from the doctor for years. Such a fool he is. He stole what we left lying around just to humor him."

"Thank you, Armond. It was something needing verification by someone other than me. There are some persons who perhaps believe I would lie to protect Mary, which is not true."

The inspector is not pleased with the information that ruins his plan to arrest my mother and possibly me. "I suppose the word of you two gentlemen will have to suffice for now. Nevertheless, I assure you that the woman will be closely watched. Someday she will find the treatment in our prison not nearly as pleasant as in your home."

"Make as many threats as you wish, Asid. I would be quite surprised if you find a valid reason to put Mary or her son behind bars."

"Humph, I would like nothing more than to surprise you. We shall see what the future holds for the wife of Osigian Nighosian and the one they call a prince of Armenia."

Dr. Demirr avoids having the conversation continue to deteriorate. He addresses an earlier offer of assistance from his friend. "Just two matters if you don't mind, Armond."

"Yes, anything you wish."

"I will appreciate your asking Mary to join me in the study, and you might as well have Nishan come, too. She does not keep matters from her son.

"Yes, sir, I will be happy to tell Miss Mary. It gives me an opportunity to say goodbye to her. The other matter, sir?"

"Yes, I believe Constantinople will not be very accommodating to Ishmail from now on. Perhaps you could take him with you."

"Oh, sir, the Turkish Army has little need for gardeners, but we can always use more men in the trenches. I will see to it that our Ismail has a good view of the battleground." The good-natured sergeant is about to exit when he comes to attention and gives a salute. Dr. Demirr follows protocol and returns the salute with a special footnote, "Goodbye, my dear friend."

I rush from the hallway to the other room just as Armond exits the study. I worry that he caught a glimpse of me darting into the room, but he makes no mention of it when he tells me to join Mother in the study. Perhaps this secret will remain between Armond and me.

~~~~~~~~~~~~~~~~~~~~~~~~

"You wish to speak with us, sir?" Mother asks when we enter the study. She avoids being startled because I have already cautioned her about the visitor.

"Mary, I thank you and Nishan for joining us. I believe you are already acquainted with our new inspector. He believes that you have stolen items from the house." Mother remains silent. Her glaring eyes are focused on an enemy of the Armenian people.

"Sir, it is not true. Surely you do not believe that I would steal from you?"

"You are correct, Mary. I don't believe it for a moment. Armond and I have already identified the real thief." Asid is disturbed at being put on the spot, but an explanation continues. "I requested your presence because I believe one has the right to confront her accuser. Do not be afraid. You are safe in my house." The inspector is trapped in an embarrassing situation. To exit abruptly will appear as though an Armenian woman got the best of him. Mother seizes the opportunity to speak for an entire nation.

"Thank you for your consideration, but I do not have the words to express my contempt for a man who butchers innocent people. My holy book tells me there is a heaven and a hell." She points directly at Asid and finishes her statement. "This devil will occupy the place in hell." Asid is humiliated. He rises from the chair to confront my mother, but Dr. Demirr halts his advance. I am ashamed that I did not act sooner to also protect her.

"Mary, I believe you expressed yourself quite admirably. You and Nishan are welcome to leave if you have nothing else to say."

Mother is not ready to leave and approaches Asid. A question has been on her mind since being rescued from the death march. "I wish to know what has become of my friends, Arixie Enjaian and Mr. Yeghesian. Do you even remember them?"

Asid is slow to answer. His eyes shift to Dr. Demirr who has the look of a courtroom prosecutor.

An evil look appears on the butcher's face. "Yes, I am familiar with the two you speak of; the tall carpet merchant and the woman who was a constant nuisance. She tormented my soldiers so much that we had to gag her. That is, until the escape."

"Escape? You mean to tell me Yeggi and Arixie got away?"

"It was only temporary," Asid responds, seemingly delighted to share the information. "It appears they outsmarted no one but themselves."

"You've gone this far, now stop stalling and tell us what happened to the two friends," Dr. Demirr says in an irritated tone.

The inspector is in no hurry. He leans back in his chair and strikes a match to light a stubby cigarette. After a few drawn out puffs of smoke, he shares the story:

Three days following Mary and Nishan's departure from the death march, the rest of the deportees are subjected to an allotment of only half-rations as punishment for the doctor's charitable act. The remaining Armenians are starving to death with at least one out of every twenty being left behind each day along the roadside as food for wild animals.

Asid says that Yeggi was very cunning. When they were camped one night near a stream, he managed to gather tiny pebbles which he rubbed until they looked like small gems that lacked color. He engaged the camp cook in a game of skambil and took his winnings in cooking ingredients which he used to concoct a gold coloring. By daylight, the pebbles looked like gold nuggets. He used the 'gold' to bribe three Kurdish guards who were planning to abandon Asid's forces. On a night when the sky was overcast, Arixie and Yeggi left the camp with the deserters.

"Thank the Lord!" Mother calls out when she hears the news. Her celebration is premature.

"Escaping is one thing; surviving is another!" The offensive outburst indicates there is more to the story. Mother grows anxious while Asid takes his time pressing the half-smoked cigarette into an ashtray. He continues only when satisfied that the intrigue has been stretched to the limit.

"A squad of soldiers was sent to search for the deserters and the two Armenian escapees. At one point, however, the group being pursued separated. My men caught up with the deserters and before they were beheaded, they confessed how Arixie and Yeggi were able to trick them with the 'fools' gold.'"

"So, you killed the deserters, but what about the two Armenians?" Dr. Demirr asks. Mother and I remain silent throughout the telling of the story but now she speaks up.

"Yes, what has happened to my friends? You say they parted from the Kurds, so perhaps they are safe."

Asid chooses to inflict more mental anguish. "No one can survive in the desert for long with very little food and water. For sure, their bones are rotting under the sun as I speak."

"I think we have heard enough, Asid," Dr. Demirr insists.

"I am merely telling the truth unlike the foolish Armenians who cling to a faith that promises there is a heaven."

"I said that's enough, Asid! If you continue, it will be you who will be praying for an afterlife."

"Doctor, I believe you are threatening me."

"Believe what you wish, but if you continue such mental torture, I will have a private conversation with your superior officer." The added pressure seems to work; Asid decides it is best to shift his attention to lighting another cigarette.

"Mary are you alright?" the doctor asks while taking hold of her hand.

"Yes, sir," she answers as tears fill her eyes. "Nishan and I should return to our rooms if you have no further need of us."

"Yes, of course, and take as much time as you need. I will be thinking of you, Mary."

The upsetting session appears to be over, but Asid's taunting continues as we exit the room. He yells an eerie warning. "You may sense a victory today, Mary Nighosian, but I will haunt you forever. You and the boy will never leave Constantinople alive!"

~~~~~~~~~~~~~~~~~~~~~~~~

Mother does return to her room, but I linger outside the study just long enough to overhear Dr. Demirr direct a question at Asid. "Tell me, Asid, why do you hate the Armenian woman so much?"

The question regarding my mother is too personal for me not to stick around to hear the answer. I remain outside the room and listen. It involves my people so I intend to hear his answer; even with the risk of being discovered. Dr. Demirr is sitting comfortably behind his desk.

"Evidently you are not aware of my prior encounters with her husband." Asid's response comes with a hateful sneer.

"Evidently not, but I am willing to listen."

"And so, you shall, my friend." It is a false gesture of affection that is quickly disregarded. Asid rises from his chair and leans his torso onto the doctor's desk. He inches forward until the hideous result of a severe wound is fully displayed only two feet from where Dr. Demirr sits. I lean closer to the slit in the door to see the inspector use his forefinger to trace the full length of the scar. He starts at the left ear which is missing its upper curvature, then passing across his eye and nose, and cutting across the corner of his mouth. The wound continues downward thru the chin until it ends halfway down the neck.

"More than two hundred sutures! That is what it took to sew my face back together. Another inch or two and he would have sliced my jugular vein. This grotesque face is what I have to show from my battle with Osigian Nighosian. It is a daily reminder of how much I hate the Armenians."

"I am moved by your story; however, I was led to believe that Mary's husband was killed."

"Yes, that came later at Amasia. A small band of Armenians engaged us on the outskirts of the village. The fools thought they could defeat an entire regiment of our forces. We outnumbered them forty to one, and still they charged our guns and cannons." He shakes his head, bewildered by the Armenian suicide mission.

"Brave men," Dr. Demirr interjects.

"Brave fools as far as I am concerned," Asid counters.

"Mary's husband was one of men who fell at Amasia?"

"Yes, I came upon him lying on the ground wounded. I pumped three bullets into him to end his suffering." Dr. Demirr shakes his head in disgust as Asid continues to recount the story. "Osigian Nighosian was a fine commander and a formidable warrior. In the end he was like any other Armenian, praying to his God for acceptance into heaven. Now, do you understand that the happiest day in my life will be when I rid this world of Mary

Nighosian and her son?" Dr. Demirr has heard enough.

"Asid, I think that the happiest day in your life may have been when Mary's husband chose to slice your face, rather than to plunge his sword into your dark heart."

I go to my room still hearing Asid's words ringing in my ears and filling my heart with sadness. I regret having listened to the account of my father's last moments. *Is losing one's life fighting for a noble cause worth the sacrifice? Evidently my father thought so.*

Note: On June 28, 1919, The Treaty of Versailles is signed by Germany. It comes exactly five years after the assassination of Archduke Franz Ferdinand which directly led to World War I. (Wikipedia: Timeline of World War I)

Chapter 31
Early 1917

Nearly a year has passed since the fateful reception at the Demirr residence. The hateful Asid uses his authority as an inspector for the gendarmes to exact personal revenge on the Armenian nation. His duties include arresting persons who attempt to escape the country by way of the port at Constantinople. The arrest is merely a formality. When it involves an Armenian, execution soon follows.

Asid continues to harass Mother whenever there is an opportunity. Twice he orders her arrest for supposed theft at the marketplace. He probably hopes she will try to escape and be shot by the arresting officers, but she refuses to fall into the trap. There is no stealing and she offers no resistance to the gendarmes. Dr. Demirr provides proof showing the charges are false and she is freed on both occasions. Now, Asid expands his list of enemies to include the good doctor. Something must be done to stop him.

My work at the household varies. The staff knows that I am available wherever help is needed. There are grounds to maintain, vehicles to clean, floors to polish, and always an abundance of dust to eliminate due to keeping large windows open for cooling purposes. Today, I work in Dr. Demirr's study. It is a fascinating room, comfortable and inviting. Two Queen Anne chairs and a small coffee table rest in front of a fireplace that provides warmth during cold months. Bookshelves filled with medical journals and classical novels line the walls. The doctor's desk is the result of finely-skilled craftsmen. I keep it highly polished. Before I leave this room, my image will reflect from the desktop.

Dr. Demirr spends much of his leisure time in the study, although his free time is less now that war casualties have continued to increase at the hospital. I think the Ottomans are losing the conflict. The war is now into the fourth year. Boasting of a swift victory by leaders of Germany and the Ottoman Empire ended long ago.

The study is a good room for conducting business, but I believe its best use is when the doctor finds time to relax and perhaps meditate. During those 'quiet' times' my mother makes sure there is coffee and tasty halvah available in the study.

My work is nearly over. Only the desk remains to be dusted and polished. I begin the task, and something catches my eye in the partially-opened middle drawer. His holstered gun is standard issue for officers of the Ottoman Army. I last saw it when he used it the day we came under attack following our rescue from the death march. I remember that he remarked how odd it is that the gun is manufactured in the United States of America, a country that is close to entering the war against the Ottoman Empire.

Mother is busy in the kitchen and the doctor left earlier to work at the hospital. I am alone and surrender to temptation. My eyes remain fixed on the gun as my hand cautiously slides the drawer fully open. I release the strap securing the gun and free it from the holster. It is heavier than expected. The ammunition clip is inserted and fully loaded. One flick of the safety mechanism and this gun is ready to kill. I wonder why Dr. Demirr believes it necessary to have a loaded weapon readily accessible in his desk. That is not my most pressing thought. At this moment, I am holding something capable of forever removing Asid from our lives.

"What do you intend to do with that handgun, young man?" The voice coming from the doorway startles me. Dr. Demirr glares at me, and he is not smiling.

"Uh, I was just..."

"Just rummaging through my desk, Nishan?"

"No, sir. The drawer was open. I saw your gun and..."

"And you were curious. Am I right?"

Lying will only make matters worse, so I shamefully mumble a weak excuse. "I only wanted to see how it felt in my hand."

He approaches me and puts a gentle hand on my shoulder. I see no anger in his face. The wise man knows this is an important moment in our relationship. "Nishan, you need to understand a few things." He gestures for me to be seated and I offer to hand over the gun. He declines and allows the weapon to be in my lap while he speaks. "This gun is not a toy. It is to be secured at all times; that is, unless you intend to shoot someone." His serious tone assures me that he is not making a joke. "You are also violating a trust when you snoop through my desk." I show a confused look that brings a quick response. "It means that I trust you with my possessions, even when I am not here." I sniffle and try to hold back tears, but there is no use. I am ashamed for having not lived up to the man's expectations. He hands me a tissue to wipe my eyes. A response from me is warranted.

"What is my punishment, sir?" I ask with trembling lips. The sincere response produces a slight smile from my lecturer.

"That is a good question, young man. If you are to be punished, then I must join you." His comment confuses me; a clarification follows. "It was I who left the drawer open and put temptation in your path. Yes, I share the blame." I realize the doctor is trying to make things better between us. He ends the session on a positive note. "This is a good lesson for both of us, so we should agree that it will not occur again." He extends a hand, and I am happy to vigorously seal the agreement.

"Thank you, sir. I promise you will never have to worry about trusting me."

217

"I already know that, Nishan. Otherwise, why would I let you sit there with a loaded gun during our conversation?" He makes a good point.

I believe our meeting is ended and I attempt to return the weapon, but the doctor is not finished. He asks me to remain seated and then brings up a sensitive topic.

"There is one other thing, Nishan. I suspect your intention went beyond just examining the weapon. If that's the case, perhaps we should talk further."

"Doctor, I am not ashamed to admit I thought about using the gun on Asid." He says nothing while considering how to deal with the matter. I nervously shift in my seat.

"Alright, this is your issue, so you can decide about Inspector Asid." He flippantly waves a hand in the air as though it makes no difference whatsoever to him. "However, keep in mind that your actions will have an impact on your future and that of other people."

"I wish for no one else to get hurt. I only want to kill Asid." My bitter words are truthful, but shallow. I sense that he is becoming frustrated that I fail to acknowledge the gravity of the situation.

"Okay, you can take that gun today and use it for the purpose of murder." I find the term cold and impersonal, just as the doctor intended. "You might even get lucky, although I imagine you will accidently shoot yourself before getting off a shot at Asid. Have you considered the consequences?" The intent to embarrass me works and remaining silent is not an option. "Well, Nishan, I am waiting for a response, even if it takes the rest of the afternoon." He leans back in the chair as though he is willing to wait me out.

I search for something intelligent to say but nothing comes to mind, so I blurt out the truth. "Consequences? I didn't even plan how to go about doing it." He nods as though my response was anticipated.

"Okay, now we are getting somewhere. Let's assume you really do succeed in killing Asid, even though we know that is quite unlikely. You have never fired a Model 390 Browning pistol in your life, or any other handgun for that matter." I am embarrassed, but he speaks the truth. "You would be arrested and go to the gallows for killing one of Constantinople's gendarmes. More accurately, you would be an Armenian that assassinated a Turk."

"Our people will be better off if he is no longer living."

"You miss my point. There are consequences to every action we take." The doctor's words become more intense. "My colleagues in the medical field face it every time we open a soldier's body to dig out a bullet or bomb fragment. Consequences can be a matter of life or death."

"I'm sorry, Dr. Demirr. I wasn't thinking about those things." The apology produces no sympathy.

"That's right; you were selfish to consider only yourself."

"I don't understand. You say I was selfish?"

"Yes, you never gave a thought to what this foolish act would do to your mother. The executioner will make swift work of your death, but you would be the one who sentenced Mary to a lifetime of grief." He pokes a finger into my chest, but it is the words that pierce my heart.

"You're right; I should have kept Mother foremost in my thoughts."

"It is not only your mother who should have been considered."

"Who else?" I innocently ask. The answer comes with a look of disappointment.

"I think the Ottoman military would frown on one of its officers carelessly allowing his sidearm to fall into the hands of someone who murdered an inspector of the gendarmes. Did you ever consider the consequence might be a court-martial for me, my would-be assassin?" No response is necessary. Dr. Demirr can see the look of regret on my face.

"Is there any more you wish to tell me, sir?" The intense conversation has tired me, and I imagine he feels the same. It is a painful, but valuable lesson.

"I don't think so, Nishan. You can either leave this room with the gun or walk out of here with a clear conscience."

I find it hard to believe that he is giving me a choice. The challenge plays tricks with my thoughts: *Will he really allow me to leave with his weapon knowing how I intend to use it? Perhaps the doctor is running a bluff only to test me.*

We sit looking at each other – a bewildered youth trying to be a man, and an adult hoping to save a young life. I think of my parents and the sacrifices they have made for me.

"Thank you, Dr. Demirr. I will not need this anymore." Then, I carefully hand the gun to the man who may have saved my life – again.

~~~~~~~~~~~~~~~~~~~~~~~~~

I lie in my bed that evening recounting the incident earlier in the day. Mother enters my room to say goodnight. She hugs me and sees the tears in my eyes.

"Nishan, is something wrong?"

"No, everything is fine... I love you, Mother."

Note: The Treaty of Sevres is signed on August 10, 1920, as a post-war pact between Allied powers and Ottoman Turkey. This treaty abolished the Ottoman Empire and called for establishing an independent Republic of Armenia. (Wikipedia: Timeline of World War I)

Chapter 32

April 1917

Dr. Demirr requests that selected members of the household and hospital staff join him in the study for an announcement. Mother and I attend the meeting along with eight others who crowd into the small room. Some are seated while others stand, but we all share a common distinction. None are Turks; the nationalities represented have all been oppressed by the Ottomans. There are Greeks, Syrians, and Armenians. If it were not for the doctor, none of us would be alive today. He addresses the group while standing next to the fireplace.

"I asked you here to share news that may have an impact on each of you." It is not often that the man speaks in such a serious tone. People give one another a worried look. "My friends, I regret to inform you that the war is escalating due to recent events." The room grows quiet as we carefully listen to an explanation. "Some weeks ago, a German submarine torpedoed and sank the British ship *S.S. California* off the coast of Ireland. Many American passengers and crew were killed when the ship went down. That incident, coupled with the discovery of a secret communication that Germany has offered Mexico certain American territories if it declares war on the United States, has triggered the

Americans to declare war on Germany." There is much talk spreading through the room as people speculate about what the future may bring. One person asks the question that is on everyone's mind.

"Doctor how will this affect us?"

"I do not have a crystal ball, but I believe the Axis Powers will come to regret America's entry into the war."

"Well, they certainly waited long enough!" a voice in the room calls out. "This war has gone on since 1914. It seems like the Americans could have made the decision years ago!"

Dr. Demirr tells the group that the Americans have previously provided the Allied countries with military supplies and weapons without making a formal declaration of war. Others in the room mention food and medical aid coming from the country across the Atlantic Ocean.

"Do you really think the Americans will make that much of a difference? It's such a young country," another person adds to the discussion.

"I certainly do," the doctor answers. People quiet down and listen to the man who understands international politics more than anyone in the group. "Yes, the United States is considered a young country based on historical records. The fact is, America already has a history steeped with military engagements. During its one hundred and forty-one years of existence, the country has fought three major wars, and one of those was between its northern and southern states." He looks directly at the people assembled before him. "Yes, my friends, I predict the Americans will turn the tide and we will soon hear their battle hymn as they come onto our shores."

This is welcomed news. There are lively conversations about what may come to pass if the Allies succeed in winning the war. Surely, freedom from oppression will be one of the greatest rewards. One person remains silent as the others celebrate. Dr. Demirr believes that his words may be construed as treason by the Ottoman leaders. Perhaps he has said too much.

The meeting adjourns, and people exit while continuing to discuss the exciting news. Dr. Demirr remains at the fireplace contemplating a war that he detests. On other occasions, the glowing embers offered a well-deserved rest from a hectic surgery schedule. Today is different. World events have taken a toll on the man who merely wanted to have a successful career and nurture a wonderful family. There is little that can take his mind off the human tragedy that grips the world.

Another person in the room also had simple dreams that were shattered. Unbeknownst to the doctor, she stayed when the others left. Now she joins him at the fireplace.

"Doctor, may I speak with you?"

"Oh, Mary, I didn't realize anyone was still here."

"I'm sorry. I did not mean to startle you. You seemed to be in deep thought."

"It's quite alright. I was just reminiscing for a moment. Is there something you need?"

"I wish to ask you something."

"Yes, I'm listening." She pauses to think about how to properly phrase the question. It is a sensitive matter. "Come now, Mary. After everything we have been through, there's not much to hold back from each other." The encouragement helps to ease her concern.

"You indicated that the Ottomans might lose the war. If that happens, is it possible that Nishan and I will no longer have to live in Constantinople?"

"I would ask you a question before attempting to answer yours, Mary." Mother is receptive, and he proceeds. "Is it that you are not happy with this arrangement?"

"Please do not think that we are not grateful. You have been wonderful." She lowers her head and makes a heartfelt confession. "We miss Armenia, and we miss our people."

Mother has learned a great deal about Dr. Demirr during our time with him. The man is not spontaneous when it comes to matters requiring deep thought. This is one of those moments. She sits quietly as he considers the matter. It is not long until he shares his thoughts.

"Mary, I know the heartbreak that forever lingers when one suffers the loss of people they love.

For you, it is not only your husband and close friends, but your entire country. I promise you that if there is any way to reunite you with your people, I will see that it happens."

The verbal commitment is overwhelming. She expresses her appreciation and rushes to tell me about her conversation with Dr. Demirr. It sounds too good to be true.

"Do you really believe we might again live as free people?" I ask. Her answer gives me hope.

"Yes. Dr. Demirr is a man of his word."

~~~~~~~~~~~~~~~~~~~

November 1917

Not much has changed in the household during the eight months since the meeting in the library. Mother and I continue with our work. Dr. DeMirr remains busy treating the wounded, and the ever-present Asid continues to threaten our lives. The outside world is changing. The doctor's prediction that the United States of America would alter the course of the war comes true. American reinforcements bring about victories in several engagements. Inspired by the increase of troops from across the ocean, the British launch a major offensive on the Western Front.

One month later, Dr. Demirr requests that Mother and I join him in the library. The news is bittersweet.

"It is important that you two remain inside the house until things settle down in Constantinople. There may be retaliations," he tells us. Mother grips my hand and braces for the news. "The British have captured Jerusalem. Your holy city is no longer under Turkish rule." This is wonderful news, but Mother cautions me to not overreact. Dr. Demirr's religious belief is different from ours. He follows the teachings of the Prophet Mohammed. I usually just listen to the adults discussing such matters, but today I am drawn into the discussion.

"Nishan, I am curious to know how you feel about all of this." The doctor has never asked for my opinion on anything, let alone world politics. I am not prepared to respond and look to Mother for assistance. None is forthcoming. I have grown older; she expects me to answer for myself. The words do not come.

"You will not offend me if you speak your mind," Dr. Demirr tells me. His soft voice reminds me of my father and the words come easier.

"Well, sir, I think there is a difference between people waging war against one another, and those who just have different beliefs about their religion. The important thing is that we believe in a Higher Power. You have your faith and I have mine. That doesn't make either of us a bad person. That's what my mother and father taught me, and I believe they're right." I hunch my shoulders and give a sheepish glance at Mother. She seems satisfied with my response.

The doctor peers over eyeglasses that have slipped lower on his nose. It is usually a sign that he is in deep thought. Time passes, and I begin to worry, but Mother gives a look telling me to have patience. Finally, his response comes accompanied with a smile.

"Nicely said, young man. Your parents have taught you well."

~~~~~~~~~~~~~~~~~~~~~~~~~~~~

Early November 1918

One year after the fighting for the Western Front, Germany signs an armistice with the Allies. World War I is over. The capital of the Ottoman Empire is in turmoil. Turkish officials scurry to relate information to the estimated one million inhabitants of Constantinople. We are among the many captured nationalities that have been detained by the Ottomans for years. Our lives are about to change.

Dr. Demirr meets with each member of the staff who were allowed to serve in a household rather than being sent to the death camps. We are the last to confer with the man who has become a friend.

"This is certainly a much different conversation," he tells us when we learn of our freedom. "I no longer have any right to keep you here." He retrieves a handkerchief from his suit pocket and whisks away a tear. "I shall miss both of you."

"Thank you for the kind words," Mother tells him.

I cannot help wondering where we are going. Reports already tell us that Amasia is a skeleton of the quaint village we left three years ago. Arixie, Yeggie, and other friends are no longer a part of our lives. Mother knows there is nothing left for us in Amasia. She shares the reality with Dr. Demirr. His response comes softly, but clearly understood.

"You can always remain here if you care to."

Note: The new First Republic of Armenia takes control of eastern Turkey after engaging Turkish troops in battle. Eventually, Turkey defeats the Armenians. This action will play a major role in Armenia losing its independence following WWI. (Wikipedia: Turkish/Armenian War

Chapter 33
Mid-November 1918

I find that Dr. Demirr's prediction comes true by listening to him read aloud the daily news reports that arrive at the house. Less than eighteen months after entering the war, the Americans tip the scales. Countries that had been overrun by invaders during the early stages of the war are liberated. The price of freedom is costly. The monetary amount takes a toll on every country's economic base and the loss of life is staggering. Thousands upon thousands of young men and women in uniform are buried in foreign soil. The loss of civilian lives is far greater. This 'war to end all wars' is a tragic period in history.

Constantinople becomes a different place now that French troops have arrived. The British come one day later followed by Italian troops not long afterward. The capital of Turkey, ruled by the Ottomans for centuries, is now divided into zones that come under the direction of troops from three Allied countries. It is the first time the city has been ruled by people other than the Ottomans since the year 1453.

We continue to reside in Dr. Demirr's home. Most of the other 'freed' workers are now gone. They left to begin new lives in countries they never dreamed to visit. Those of us who stayed had little choice. Our villages, families, and lifestyles were decimated when the Turks invaded our country.

I listen to adults discussing what changes may occur in the world now that the capital city is under new leadership. Their concerns are not as personal as mine, however I soon learn that not everything changes when a war comes to an end.

"Unfortunately, we must continue to deal with the man, at least for time being," Dr. Demirr tells me when I inquire about Inspector Asid. "The Allied leaders have chosen to have the gendarmes continue serving as the local police force." The alarming news upsets me.

"Why would they do such a thing? Everyone in Constantinople other than the Turks will continue to be persecuted. Nothing has changed!" The doctor ignores my outburst and tries to bring a voice of reason into the discussion.

"It is politics, Nishan. Most likely there is an agreement which helps the Ottoman leaders retain a bit of honor in defeat. Gendarmes patrolling the city streets will project a sense of sovereignty. It may help to keep the citizens calm during this change in power."

"I don't believe keeping Inspector Asid around is going to have a calming effect on the people," I angrily respond.

"I understand your feelings, Nishan. Nevertheless, if you are to have enemies, it is best to know who they are. It is the unknown enemy you must fear the most."

I will follow the learned man's advice. This new-found freedom does not mean one can let his guard down.

~~~~~~~~~~~~~~~~~~~~~~~~~~~

December 1919

It has been one year since the end of World War I. We enjoy a Constantinople that is stabilized by the occupying forces. Treaties are signed between various countries. The local gendarmes attempt to keep the peace, but there is friction between them and soldiers from other nations. The gendarmes represent law enforcement in Constantinople, but the foreign troops are a constant reminder that the Turks no longer rule the city. Inspector Asid does not help matters with his continual torment of Armenians who remain in Constantinople. For him, the war is not over.

There are some positive changes in my life. I have more responsibility within the household and adjacent hospital, although it is a much slower pace now that there are no longer wounded soldiers filling the rooms. I am paid a wage for my work. While somewhat meager, it does provide extra money to spend in the market shops. Another change is with my education. Mother and Dr. Demirr agree that I should receive formal schooling. She has done a good job teaching me letters and numbers. However, learning materials have been sparse.

There is now an opportunity for me to become better-educated. New schools have been created in the city. Some are staffed by the nuns of the Catholic faith. I attend their classes for three hours each morning where I learn about different languages and cultures of the world. This is when I become familiar with America. I find it interesting to study the country consisting of many separate states that answer to a common federal government. Its geography is fascinating - mountains, plains, deserts, roaring rivers, and men called cowboys. The language is not easy. Some words sound the same but have different meanings.

My life exists in Constantinople, but the nuns tell me that by learning the English language, I will become worldlier, so I learn to count the numbers. Now the Armenian *meg, yergoo, yerek, and chors* become one, two, three and four. The *jur* we take from the mountain springs is referred to as water in English. Sometimes I become confused by the words and revert to my native language. It is then that the nuns rap my knuckles with a measuring stick and say, "Speak English; you may need it some day!"

My response is trite. "When will I ever need to speak English? I am halfway around the world from America."

Note: July 24, 1923. The Treaty of Lausanne cancels the Treaty of Sevres and Armenia loses its independent status as a nation. This leaves Armenia open to invasion by Turkey and Russia." (Wikipedia: Timeline of World War I)

Chapter 34

February 1920

It is an ordinary day, but that is all about to change. Mother and I are cleaning the study when Dr. Demirr walks in after receiving the morning mail delivery. He takes a seat at his desk and begins thumbing through the stack of letters and publications. One item seems unusual.

"Mary, this envelope may be intended for you," he says while examining the posted address. "It has my address, but your name is highlighted." He hands her the tattered envelope that shows signs of having been opened and crudely resealed. She gives the doctor a questioning look. "Yes, I noticed it, too. Perhaps someone connected with the gendarmes is screening the mail."

"Asid?" Mother questions.

"I can't imagine why Inspector Asid would have reason to snoop through mail coming to this house from America," he answers, pointing to the return address. "I'm just as curious as you. Go ahead and open it."

I welcome the break in our work and plop myself in a cushioned chair. Dr. Demirr raises an eyebrow but does not verbally object to my familiarity with his furnishings.

Mother pulls back the edges of the envelope and retrieves a single sheet of paper containing a message. Her eyes tear up when she recognizes the handwriting. She slowly lowers herself onto the sofa and does a second reading of the short note. It is written by someone who disappeared from our lives more than four years ago.

"Is it bad news?" the doctor inquires. Mother can barely speak as the tears stream down her cheeks and drip onto the note. She is overwhelmed, but not distraught. Dr. Demirr hands her a tissue which she uses to carefully pat the note and absorb the moisture. It is obvious that this small document is dear to her.

"No, not bad news," she tells us between deep breaths. "It is wonderful news. I will share it with you." She continues to dab her eyes and reads:

My Dear Mary,

I hope this letter reaches you and that you are safe. My earlier letters did not find you due to the the war.

I remembered that the doctor who took you and young Nishan from the death march was on his way to Constantinople. A Red Cross group helped me to find an address where he could be located.

I live in the United States of America. Yeggi also lives in America, but not close to me. I pray that you are alive, and this note reaches you. Please respond.

My address is: 702 Cotterell Street, Detroit, Michigan, U.S.A.

Your friend, Arixie Enjaian

"This is fantastic news. Your friends are alive after all of this time," the doctor says, shaking his head in amazement.

"Yes, it has been too long," my mother replies between sniffles.

"Well, this certainly calls for a celebration," the doctor announces in a cheerful tone. "What do you say we enjoy a glass of wine?" I eagerly rise from my chair to accept the invitation, but Mother does not like the idea.

"Nishan, sit down. The doctor was not speaking to you." Fortunately, I have a friend in the room.

"Come now, Mary. This is truly a special occasion. Surely you can allow the boy just a pinch of fruity wine. After all, he is really no longer a child."

"Well, just a pinch," Mother concedes. Dr. Demirr has already pulled a bottle and three glasses from the wine rack. He pours and manages to sneak a nearly full glass to me while Mother reads the letter for a third time. I do not hesitate to gulp down the seasoned spirits. An embarrassing belch betrays the fact that my glass held more than a pinch. Mother frowns but says nothing to spoil the joyful mood in the room.

"Ahh, now that is what I call a proper celebration!" Dr. Demirr says after emptying his glass. He gives me a slap on the back and pours himself another drink. I begin to think the man has enjoyed more than one glass of 'sweet nectar' today. He turns his attention away from me and continues to sip.

"Mary, I think you should have a seat at my desk and respond to your friend's letter right now. Here, use my ink pen and stationary." He motions for her to have a seat at his desk. This giddiness is rare, and I enjoy being a spectator. The doctor has a sense of humor that is hidden under layers of guilt due to the loss of his family. That sadness is set aside for the moment. "You write the letter and when you're finished, I will have it posted to America. Nishan and I will leave you alone in the room. Take your time." Mother expresses her appreciation as the doctor, and I are leaving the room.

"Thank you, sir. Arixie and Yeggie are like family to me."

The comment strikes close to home. We are in the hallway when he pauses at the staircase. The pleasant smile disappears as his eyes trace each agonizing step to the third floor. I do not interrupt his deep thoughts. Then he whispers to someone who is not present. "Yes, family is everything."

~~~~~~~~~~~~~~~~~~~~~~~~

Mother's letter arrives in Detroit, Michigan, four weeks after being posted from Constantinople. Arixie's reply takes another month to cross the Atlantic Ocean and travel through the Mediterranean Sea. It is confiscated when reaching the port of Constantinople. Delivery is delayed for three days before it is delivered to the house.

I am anxious to learn what Arixie has written, but first Mother carefully examines the envelope. Someone has done a better job of disguising the fact that this letter was opened after its voyage across the ocean. Only a sliver of tape makes it appear the envelope was accidently torn in transit, but she believes otherwise. Some person is very interested in her communications from America.

"Nishan, come sit with me. I wish to share this letter from Arixie." I rush to her side, anxious to hear the news coming from the woman I have come to know as my aunt Arixie:

Dear Mary,

My prayers were answered when your letter arrived. There is much to tell you.

I am married to a wonderful man. His name is Dakes Sarkisian. Our home in Detroit is in an area called Delray. It contains many of our Armenians. The Polish and Greek people live in nearby neighborhoods. We often ask our Greek friends why they insist on calling our delicious pastry baklava instead of paklava. Those crazy Greeks, always wanting to be different!

Mary, the prediction you made that day when all hope for survival was lost has come true. Dakes and I will have children. The first

239

little girl will be named Vartanoush. She will be our 'Sweet Rose'.

Our friend, Yeggi, helped me to escape the Turks after that cruel sergeant threatened to have his men rape our women if we would not walk in the desert without food or water. We made it to Marseilles, France. An organization put us in touch with Armenians who fled to other countries during the war.

There are Armenian men who desire to marry again after losing their wives during the war. These men offer to sponsor Armenian women to the United States to begin a new life and continue the bloodline. If you wish, I will have someone contact you about coming to America.

I will end for now. You may be thousands of miles away, but you are always close to my heart. Tell Nishan that I long to hug him and tell his future from the coffee cup once again.

Forever your friend, Arixie

"Mother, it is so far away. Are you really thinking about having us go to America?"

"I need time to think about this," she answers with a worried look. "There is more to consider than just myself." She has spent years suffering from abuse by the Turks, and now she deserves to be completely free of it.

"This is an opportunity for you to begin a new life. What else is there to consider?"

Her thoughtful answer comes quickly. "I will think about what is best for you, my prince."

Note: Ancient Armenian churches contained distinct architectural features: Pointed domes reminiscent of the volcanic dome of Mt. Ararat, vaulted ceilings, tall and narrow windows, ornate frescos and carvings, and tall structural arches. (Wikipedia: Medieval Armenian Churches)

Chapter 35

May 1920

Mother and Arixie continue to correspond as they renew their long-time friendship. Each letter arriving from America encourages us to make the voyage across the Atlantic Ocean. Mother is hesitant. She knows it means we will never return to our beloved Armenia.

One thing in Arixie's favor for reuniting with us is that Armenia is still in a state of unrest. The nation's fate is unknown following the war. Mother is close to making a commitment to America when an international event causes her to reconsider. It also triggers her first argument with Dr. Demirr since we joined him years earlier.

~~~~~~~~~~~~~~~~~~~~~~~~~~~~~~

August 1920

"I see your people finally got their wish," the doctor tells us when he enters a room that Mother and I have been cleaning this morning. We stop our work and he hands her a newspaper that he has been reading. I sit down in a freshly-dusted chair but she remains standing while reading an article aloud. The news story gives an account of a treaty crafted in Sevres, France, by the victorious Allied countries.

"Nishan, this is good news. The Allies have agreed to establish a free state of Armenia near Yerevan. Armenia will be an independent nation once again!" It is a happy moment and I hurry to give my mother a hug. Dr. Demirr is not as jubilant.

"Pardon me if I do not join in the celebration," he says in a disappointed tone. "That treaty calls for several territories to be separated by Turkey. It will spell the end of the Ottoman Empire as we now know it."

"And is that so bad?" Mother asks. "Much of that land did not belong to Turkey in the first place. It was acquired from the blood of many innocent people."

The statement shocks me. Her words are true and spoken in anger. Perhaps she has failed to consider our host. Dr. Demirr has always remained faithful to his country, even though he shows kindness to those who do not follow the Islamic faith. His anger shows.

"Mary, I am surprised that you now chastise the people who protected the Armenians when Russia tried to take over your country. If it were not for the Ottoman Empire, Armenia would have been ruled by the Emperor of Russia!" The defense of his country is honorable, but it does not set well with Mother.

"Yes, and perhaps it would be better to live under Russian rule than to die from a Turkish saber!"

It is difficult for me to witness this debate between two people that care so much for each other. Dr. Demirr's suppressed anger is erupting like a volcano, and Mother is not her usual congenial self. They stare at one another unwilling to back down in their beliefs.

"Mother, please, no more! The two of you are scaring me!" My shouts grab their attention and the mood in the room gradually changes. Uncontrolled anger turns to embarrassment as both parties try to gain their composure. No one speaks for a few moments, but there are obvious signs of sadness. Mother breaks the silence.

"Sir, I am sorry for my words; they were spoken in anger. It will not happen again." Her eyes remain focused on the oriental carpet. I am worried that too much damage has been done. Perhaps the relationship is forever broken. It takes only seconds for me to learn the measure of an honorable man. Dr. Demirr places a hand under Mother's chin and raises her head to make eye contact.

"There is no need to apologize, Mary. Both of us were caught up in a battle of cultures. You have your beliefs, and I have mine. What matters is that we continue to respect one another." He smiles, and all is well between the two of them.

"Thank you, sir. You are a good man. Nishan and I appreciate everything you have done for us." The compliment is touching and causes our friend to recall something very personal. We allow him time to sort through his thoughts. When he speaks, the words come from his heart.

"It is I who should thank the two of you. Years of guilt have haunted me since I lost my wife and children. I sacrificed them for a cause that was far less important than their safety. If I had been here, they might still be with me." The personal confession is too emotional, and he chokes up, unable to continue.

"Yes, I understand. I often wish that Nishan's father had remained with us on that day when he left for a noble cause." A sympathetic nod tells her the doctor makes the connection. She gives a final thought. "We cannot change the past, but our religion teaches that all things happen for a reason. It is called faith."

The room remains quiet as three people sit together on the couch watching the glowing embers. We have our memories.

~~~~~~~~~~~~~~~~~~~~~~~~~~~~~~

The next months are peaceful in the Demirr home. Mother and the doctor avoid what they call 'the dreaded word' and do not discuss *politics*.
She writes in her letters to Arixie that there will be a delay in the decision regarding coming to America. We are hopeful that the new nation of Armenia will become a reality as promised in the Treaty of Sevres.

Note: (1914-1918, Armenian Genocide) (1918-1920, First Republic of Armenia Created) (1920, Soviet Troops Invade Armenia) (1920 and forward, Soviets Control Armenia) (1987-Present, Independence of Armenia) (2018, 100th Anniversary of the First Republic of Armenia): (Wikipedia: Armenia Timeline)

Chapter 36

November 1920

Although the Treaty of Sevres brings hope that someday we will return to a new Armenia, I come to realize little progress is made to implement the plan. The war may be over, but the fighting does not end. Not long after the treaty is signed, there is renewed fighting. I hear reports that the Turks and Kurds continue their attacks on the Armenian people. This time, however, the Armenians take the offensive and account for many early victories. Now the talk around the Constantinople marketplace is that the Ottomans are increasing the number of troops committed to defeating what they fear may soon become an independent nation of Armenia.

Armenians request assistance from the Allied countries, but the war took a tremendous toll on every country involved in the conflict. The Allies fail to provide aid to the Armenians. Dr. Demirr shares more disappointing news when he tells us that a request for United States President Woodrow Wilson to use his influence for establishing a free Armenia goes unfulfilled. Our dream of returning to our native country disappears, and Mother writes to Arixie about coming to America. Our friend in Detroit hurriedly responds.

"Nishan, a letter has arrived from America. It is from Arixie," She quickly opens the envelope. I take a seat in a chair and eagerly listen while she reads aloud:

Dear Mary,

Your last letter filled my heart with joyful news. I have contacted a representative of the organization that sponsors Armenian women coming to the United States.

You will receive a visit from him sometime in future weeks as he will be traveling to your Constantinople. He will interview you. If it goes well, he will connect you with an Armenian gentleman to sponsor you to America. His name is Mesak.

I count the days until we are together again. Please tell Nishan that I love him.

Your friend always, Arixie

~~~~~~~~~~~~~~~~~~~~~~~~~~~~~~

We wait for several weeks, but there is no further contact. Then, just as we are about to give up hope, a knock comes at the front door. Mother opens it and finds a short, slightly-built man she calculates to be about fifty years old. He features a nicely trimmed mustache and is attired in a tailored business suit. I listen from the hallway.

"Parev anoonus Mesak e." (Hello, my name is Mesak) He speaks perfect Armenian with a distinct accent and has a pleasant smile.

"I recognize your name," Mother tells the man, "and I understand English if you wish to speak it." Mesak hunches his shoulders and nods his head left and right indicating either language if fine with him.

"May I have the pleasure of addressing Mary Nighosian?"

"Yes, I am Mary. You are the gentleman from the Armenian organization?"

"Yes, I am pleased to make your acquaintance." He gives a courteous tip of his hat. She is not used to such an honorable gesture. Many of the men in Constantinople shun treating an Armenian woman with respect. "I apologize for not giving you more notice. There has been difficulty with my lodging and travel arrangements. Turkish officials make it difficult for me to carry out my assignments." He waves a hand to indicate the subject is not worth discussing. "Never mind, we have more important things to discuss."

"Please come inside, Mesak. I have been expecting you. We can talk in the study." He takes a moment to examine his shoes to not track in any dirt. He enters and immediately sees me. The man seems startled and looks to Mother.

"This is my son, His name is Nishan."

The man gives a courteous smile and offers a handshake. He remains cordial, but I sense something may not be right when he tells Mother, "I was not informed that you had a child, Mrs. Nighosian." He keeps his attention on Mother even as he vigorously shakes my hand.

"Yes, sir. Nishan is nearing his teen years. We are very close to each other. I would very much like for him to join us in the study. That is, if it is alright with you."

The man hesitates but avoids an awkward situation. "Yes, of course, Mrs. Nighosian.

"Thank you, and you are welcome to call me Mary." Her friendly manner lightens the mood as we enter the study.

"Yes, and everyone just calls me Mesak. Heavens, I would not know how to answer if they called me Mr. Mesak!"

Mother and Mesak slip into comfortable chairs near the fireplace. I sit on the couch. Mother has told me to be a listener unless I am to answer a question. She offers our guest some refreshment.

"Mesak, will you have some *lokma*?"

"Thank you, but I am passing up pastries for the time being," he says and pats his stomach.

"You don't appear to have a weight problem from what I can tell."

"Well, it has never been a problem until I began interviewing so many Armenian women. Now, everywhere I go, they feed me paklava, helva, lokma, boeregs, sweet targhana, and lokoom. I may be big as a dirigible by the time I return to America!"

They snicker, and it is all I can do to avoid bursting into laughter.

Mother and Mesak take some time getting to know one another; then it is time to get down to business.

"Just a few questions please," he tells Mother while retrieving a notebook from a briefcase.

"Yes, I am happy to tell you anything you wish to know."

"Thank you. This should not take long. Much of it is just a formality to comply with the organization's guidelines. Your friend, Arixie Enjaian, went through a similar interview." He starts to snicker and then breaks into a huge laugh. Mother patiently sits until he regains his composure.

"Sir is everything alright?"

"Yes, yes, I apologize. It's just that every time I think about the interview with Arixie the chuckles begin."

"Arixie tends to have that effect on people," Mother says with a smile. "I suppose she offered to tell your fortune before you left her house."

"Exactly, Mary! Oh, I must put the interview on hold to share a story with you; that is, if you don't mind."

"Yes, please. I would love to hear it if it involves my friend."

Mesak sets aside his notebook and proceeds with sharing his unique experience. "When I finished Arixie's interview, she offered to read the stains from my coffee cup to tell my future. It was a wonderful prediction! She told me that I would meet a young, beautiful and wealthy woman. We would fall in love and have many children together."

"That seems very nice to me. Were you not pleased with it?" Mother asks.

"Uh, I would say it was fifty-fifty." She gives him an inquisitive look that begs for an explanation. The entertaining gentleman is happy to comply.

"Well, I was overjoyed with my fortune, but my dear wife of twenty years was not happy when she heard that I am predicted to run off with a younger woman!" Again, the room fills with laughter and the interview is postponed longer. The humor helps to overcome a bit of anxiety and the interview moves smoothly along.

"Your name is Mary Nighosian?"

"Yes, that is my married name."

"You came from the village of Amasia in Armenia, and your husband is deceased?"

"Yes, that is correct," Mother softly answers.

"His name please?"

"Osigian. He was killed by the Turks while defending Amasia."

"Oh, I am sorry." He pauses a moment to show respect for the fallen warrior. Then, the interview proceeds. "Your age?" Mother hesitates and receives an assurance. "Not to worry, Mary. You are a lovely woman. There will be many Armenian men desiring to meet you." The compliment brings on a flash of emotion, and Mesak pauses just long enough for my mother's rosy cheeks to return to normal.

"I was born in 1890. This year marks my thirtieth birthday."

A few more questions are answered, and the formal part of the interview ends. Mesak takes a few minutes to explain how the sponsorship program works. He also describes some of the Armenian communities in the United States.

"Arixie lives in the Delray section of Detroit. It is a manufacturing city. Many Armenians work in the automobile industry."

"It is nice to know that our people find work there," Mother tells him.

"Also, in the states of California and Washington, there are miles and miles of vineyards and orchards. There are also many Armenians there." He adds an afterthought. "We seem to excel at working with nature." The information is interesting and a little confusing.

"I worry that we will have difficulty adjusting to such a diverse geography and economy."

The congenial man ends the session with a bit of flattery. "I would not be too concerned about that. You are an excellent candidate for sponsorship. We should have little difficulty matching you with a fine gentleman who will be a good provider. America will welcome such a lovely and talented woman." She accepts the compliment with humility. Mesak looks at me still seated on the couch and I see a show of concern. Mother notices it, too.

"Is there a problem, sir?"

Mesak's response is honest and to the point. "Many of the eligible men seem to prefer marriage to a woman with no children. They wish to start their own families."

"I can't imagine why Arixie did not say anything to you about my son. She loves Nishan."

"Actually, it is not that unusual. I think your friend was thinking about you. She probably feared that I would decline to interview you if I knew there was a child involved. The opportunities for sponsorship are less for women with children," he admits, while shrugging his shoulders.

"It seems so unfair. Nishan has been through so much during the war years. His maturity is far beyond his age."

"Yes, I find that to be true. He appears polite and well-mannered." Mesak gives me a pleasant smile which I appreciate since they seemed to talk as though I was not even in the room. It helps when he speaks directly to me. "I am sorry, Nishan, if this is an uncomfortable discussion for you. You needn't be worried. Arixie probably believed it would impress me if I met you in person, and she was right."

The kind words do little to ease Mother's anxiety. "Does this mean we may be excluded from the program?"

The sensitive question is answered by a compassionate man who is well-suited for the job. "Not necessarily," Mesak tells her. "It simply makes the challenge a little more difficult, but give me some time to work on this. You will be foremost in my thoughts, Mary."

I join my mother at the front door to watch the man who holds our future walk away. My nights will be filled with dreams of America, and a prayer that Mesak is successful.

Note: Henry Morgenthau, U.S. Ambassador to Turkey, resigned his post in 1916. He declared one of his reasons was to expose the conditions in the Turkish Empire, especially the harsh treatment of Armenians. (Suny: History of the Armenian Genocide)

Chapter 37

February 1921

It is several weeks since the interview with the man called Mesak. Mother remains calm, hoping for positive news. He has already sent two letters. Each contain the same message: "Mary, I continue to work on this matter for you. Have faith."

There is much activity in Constantinople. I find that not all of it is good. The Allied forces have maintained control over their respective sections of the city. This includes preventing Inspector Asid from his fixation on harassing the Armenian population. Now there comes a change. Many of the security forces are reassigned to other locations within the region. This gives Asid incentive to pursue his personal agenda.

"Nishan, I think you and your mother should be cautious about leaving the house during evening hours," the doctor tells me one morning. "Inspector Asid has ordered that any Armenians found on the streets after dark will be arrested for loitering. He claims this is to ensure that visitors from other countries are protected now that there are less Allied soldiers in the city."

"That is ridiculous," I protest to the doctor. "Armenians are not going to harm people that freed us from living under the tyranny of the Ottoman rulers." I am about to launch into a heated debate which the doctor tactfully avoids.

"I realize that Inspector Asid's accusation is without merit, but it is best to be cautious for the time being. I am told that not all gendarmes agree with his tactics." This insight turns out to be accurate.

On the following day, a lieutenant of the gendarme's countermands Asid's edict. He issues a reprimand to the inspector based on numerous reports that he has exceeded his authority, especially when dealing with matters involving the Armenian people. The lieutenant makes something clear to Asid: "One more incident and you will be the one spending time in the Constantinople prison." The commanding officer receives praise for his defense of the oppressed people, but he has made an enemy who swears to get revenge.

Another four weeks pass until we hear from Mesak. He tells us to expect a communication from a man described as a respected Armenian merchant "who does not drink to excess." The letter arrives two weeks later. Mother is eager to share it with me.

> *Dear Mary Nighosian,*
>
> *My name is Asadour Erganian. I came to America hoping to make enough money to establish a new life for my wife and children. Before I could accomplish this, my entire family*

died when the Turks invaded our village in the 'old country'. I am now all alone.

In America, I am a grocery merchant. My home is nicely furnished, and I have very little debt. My age is a young forty-three years.

I desire to meet a pleasant Armenian woman for the purpose of matrimony. I am told you have a son. He will be welcomed into my home. I have enough funds to care for you and the boy.

I would like to hear from you with the hope you have interest in this arrangement.

Respectfully, Asadour Erganian

"What do you think of this proposal?" Mother asks and sits down next to me, so our talk can be more personal.

I fumble for the right words and finally blurt out, "He seems like a nice man, but he's older than you."

"Come now, Nishan. You can do better than that. I want to know if you can accept having me be married again."

"Okay, I will be truthful and tell you that it will trouble me to consider another man to be my father."

"I respect your feelings," she says, seemingly not surprised by my response. "No one will ever replace Osigian in either of our hearts." She continues, "This man seems like a person who would not wish to diminish your love for your father." Listening to her comforting words makes it easier to accept the change. She deserves an assurance from me.

"Well, since you put it that way, I say we go to America!" My jubilance is somewhat premature. There are other concerns to discuss, but they are resolved with the help of Dr. Demirr. He is in favor of the decision and offers his assistance as we make plans.

Mother writes her reply to Asadour Erganian on the same evening. I am already in bed dreaming of America.

Note: A new Republic of Turkey is founded in 1923 and the capital is moved from Constantinople to Ankara. Constantinople is officially renamed Istanbul in 1930. (Wikipedia: Naming of Constantinople)

Chapter 38

July 1921

Mother and the gentleman from America have become more acquainted during the past months. They have shared personal thoughts intended only for each other, but other eyes at the gendarme headquarters have monitored the letters.

Now at mid-year, any doubts regarding the union are erased. Mother accepts the gentleman's proposal of marriage. Mesak's next letter comes in September and provides details:

Dear Mary Nighosian,

Arrangements are finalized for you and your son. Mr. Asadour Erganian has deposited enough money in an account for sponsorship to America. I have filed statements attesting that you are of good character and will not in any manner be a burden to the United States of America.

You and your son are to be on the ship 'Gil Djmal' when it sails from Constantinople in August of 1921. The exact day of departure will be provided to you once the cargo is loaded and secured. Have your belongings ready as your notice may be only a matter of hours.

Upon your arrival to the United States, you will enter at Ellis Island where Mr. Erganian and someone from our organization will assist you and your son with 'processing'.

I wish you and your son much happiness in your new home. May the Lord shine His light upon you.

Mesak

The good news is to be celebrated, although it comes with sadness; we must bid farewell to the man who protected us during desperate times.

During the next several weeks, Mother and I walk the two miles to the harbor where we observe the *Gul Djmal* being made ready for the long voyage. Each day, cargo is loaded into large compartments located in the bowels of the huge ship. An office at the port remains busy as people come and go booking passage to various locations where the vessel will stop along the coast of the Mediterranean Sea before entering open waters and heading to America.

Mesak's letter prompted us to gather our meager possessions. The well-to-do passengers will likely transport their belongings in large 'steamer' trunks, but we need only two satchels. This is good because many immigrants will be accommodated in the steerage level of the ship where there is little space for luggage.

Watching the ship being prepared for the voyage is exciting, but I find it comes with an anxiety to get on with it. Mother is more patient and suggests that I do the same. "You have your whole life ahead of you, Nishan. Just take one day at a time. Every day is a gift from the Lord."

Finally, the ship is ready for the journey and still no word from Mesak. I fear that we may be left behind, but a communication awaits us when we return to the house:

The Gul Djmal sails tomorrow at 9:00 a.m.
Mesak

~~~~~~~~~~~~~~~~~~~~~~~~~

That evening, we join Dr. Demirr in the study. It is our last evening with a man I greatly admire. He continues to consider our welfare.

"The ship's captain is a friend of mine," he tells us. "He will be expecting you. Contact him when you board."

"Thank you, sir," Mother responds. "I will introduce myself to him. Is there anything else I should know?"

"I think not. It is a long voyage, but there will be people watching over you. They will provide aid, if you require it." He looks to me, and his words help me to overcome the anxiety of crossing an ocean.

The mood in the cozy room becomes somber as the three of us share our last evening together. There is little conversation; the parting brings sadness. Tears form in my eyes, but Dr. Demirr will not allow this night to be remembered as anything other than a pleasant occasion.

"Come now, we will have no tears of remorse in this room. After all, it's not a morgue." Mother politely smiles, but I break into laughter at his statement intended to lighten the mood. He continues with a proposition. "I believe a toast is in order!" he announces, while stepping to the wine cabinet. There's a short lull as he surveys the variety of selections. "Well now, let's see what we have here. Perhaps a sweet red, Mary?"

"Yes, that will be fine." There is only one more thing to decide before the corkscrew is removed from the wine bottle. Dr. Demirr poses the question which I am hesitant to ask.

"Shall I pour two glasses or three?" He gives me that special wink which I have become accustomed to. Mother pretends to not see it.

"Two full ones and another with less quantity," she answers to my disappointment.

He hands each of us a glass and pours the vintage spirits that have been aged many years. Mother makes no mention of my glass having been filled to the top.

"To my friends, Mary and Nishan! I pray their journey in life is filled with as much happiness as they have given me." Three glasses touch and the friendship sealed. I enjoy the taste of fermented grapes on this evening, but it is the words that I shall savor. Mother expresses our appreciation.

"Thank you, Dr. Demirr. My son and I can never repay your kindness," Mother says, following the toast. "You protected us at great risk to your reputation, perhaps even your life."

He appears to be in deep thought as his eyes focus on the intricate patterns woven into the ornate carpet beneath our feet. We do not disturb his meditation. Then, he softly speaks.

"There is no need to praise me for doing what is right, Mary. It is I who thank the two of you for restoring my life." Mother and I remain silent as he shares his inner-most thoughts. "Grief over the loss of my wife and children consumed me. I scorned the third floor for being the place where my family died. However, seeing the two of you each day expressing such love for one another has brought about a change in me. I now believe those family rooms are filled with memories of happier times, the sounds of children laughing and a beautiful woman by my side. Yes, that is what I shall remember each time I visit the third floor."

Nightfall approaches. The fireplace provides a small measure of warmth. A cool breeze rustles the window curtains but fails to disturb three people whose friendship has been born out of tragedy.

Note: In June 1941, Nazi Germany attacks the Soviet Union. More than half a million Armenians fight on the front lines to defeat Germany. Several talented Armenian commanders make a major contribution to defeating the Nazi invasion. (Rem Ananikyan: Yerevan)

Chapter 39

I am restless during the night while anticipating the voyage. I stay awake, but my body eventually surrenders to nature. A knock on my door awakens me in a few hours. "Wake up, sleepyhead. Our ship sails in a few hours," Mother cheerfully announces.

I hurry to get dressed and head for the kitchen. Mother and Dr. Demirr are having coffee. The excitement of the day subdues my appetite, but my mother insists that I eat something, fearing the choppy seas will play havoc with my stomach. A piece of warm choreg washed down with a cup of milk will help.

It is 8:00 a.m. and time to exit the house. Dr. Demirr will take us to the harbor in his vehicle. We gather our stuffed satchels and start to leave, but already there is a problem. A shadowy figure is trying to see through the frosted glass of the front door. Our worst enemy has arrived.

"Step into the hall closet and be quick about it!" Dr. Demirr instructs us. "I will delay him inside the study. Make your way through the streets until you reach the ship. Good luck, my friends!" He closes the door behind us but leaves it slightly ajar. The narrow slit will allow us to know when it is safe to exit. I crouch down so both of us can peek through the opening.

265

Dr. Demirr waits to be sure we are safe before responding to the constant ringing of the doorbell. When it goes silent, a series of abrasive poundings on the door finally brings a response. Mother holds my hand for comfort.

"Yes, Inspector Asid, what is it you want?" The doctor gives the impression that he has just awakened. A fake yawn helps his masquerade.

"We are here to arrest the woman and her son," Asid tells him. Two gendarmes accompany the abrasive inspector.

"I will be happy to accommodate you, but first there is a matter that I wish to discuss with you and your men in private. Please join me." He leads the way to the study, but the ploy is only partially successful. The two gendarmes are ordered to stand guard outside the house. They will see us even if we try to leave through another door. We are trapped inside the closet.

Precious time is wasting away but shouting coming from the study draws our attention. Now we fear for Dr. Demirr's safety. Mother makes the decision to grab our satchels and cautiously step toward the study.

The conversation with Asid is not going well. As we listen from outside the room, it is obvious that Dr. Demirr's attempt to keep the man from persecuting Armenians has failed.

"So, you continue to protect them! Asid shouts in rage. "I am tired of your meddling in my affairs.

Perhaps you should suffer the same fate as your friends when I catch up with them!"

The threat to our friend is more than I can stand. Without thinking, I rush into the room with disregard for my safety. Mother calls for me to stop but I am already committed. She rushes after me, but it is too late. Asid has drawn his weapon.

The surprise entry causes Asid to hesitate and turn to us. Now he waves the gun wildly back and forth. First at us, then Dr. Demirr, and then back at us. The man is just crazy enough to start firing at any moment.

The distraction has given Dr. Demirr a chance to slide his hand inside the middle drawer of his desk. He feels the grip of his military pistol and his fingers inch their way to the trigger. "Killing us will do no good, Asid. You and the Ottoman Empire are finished!" Asid scoffs at the notion. His careless handling of the gun threatens to end the conversation at any movement. Dr. Demirr makes a final statement to the man who has tormented our lives for years. "The time when tyrants such as you are tolerated has come to an end. If I must sacrifice my life to stop you, then so be it." He pulls his weapon from the drawer, aims it at Asid and shouts, "Mary! Nishan! Run for it!

Asid is bewildered. If he fires at us, surely, he will take a bullet from the doctor. He stands frozen as Mother and I dash from the study and run to the front door. Our friend and protector stays behind to hold Asid at bay.

We exit the house carrying our satchels, but the guards halt us on the front steps.

"Stop right there, you two!" One gendarme detains Mother while the other places a firm hand on my shoulder. Our plans to start a new life are stalled. The men begin to escort us inside when a voice calls out from a uniformed man rushing toward us.

"Release those people!" The ranking officer shouts to the men.

The men immediately comply with the ranking officer's order and give a salute. "Yes sir, lieutenant."

"These people are free to leave. You men may return to your regular duties." The two gendarmes comply with the order. It appears we can flee, but Mother wants to express our gratitude to the lieutenant.

"Thank you, sir. It is most kind of you," she tells him.

"You are welcome, Mary." His familiarity with her name is surprising. She studies his face and finds it to be familiar. He steps closer and removes his hat. "Perhaps it's the beard. I did not have the facial hair that day at the hospital." My mother looks as though she has seen a ghost; however, her words tell me there is nothing to fear.

"Hasan, it is you!"

"Yes, Mary. It's been a few years since you comforted a young army recruit from the dizzy spells. It certainly helped prevent me from going into shock." She takes a step back to admire the man who now commands a gendarme unit in Constantinople. "Hasan how is it that you came to this house today?"

"It is not by accident," he tells her. "I have been observing Inspector Asid's activities for some time now. He clearly oversteps his authority, especially with the Armenians." We shake our heads in agreement, as Lieutenant Hasan continues. "Just this morning, I learned from an informant that Asid intends great harm to both of you before you can board the *Gul Djmal*. I am sorry that I could not arrive sooner, but he sabotaged the vehicles at our station. He must have figured out that I was on to him." The lieutenant cuts the conversation short when we hear the blast of a ship's horn coming from the port. "That is the first of three signals that come twenty minutes apart. Your ship is preparing to raise the anchor. You must hurry! Two more signals and it sails, with or without you." He quickly scribbles something on a notepad. "Take this with you. It may help if you are stopped." Mother slips the small piece of paper into her coat pocket.

"Hasan, how can we ever repay your kindness?" she asks, while giving him a hug.

"You already have, Mary... years ago."

The special moment is interrupted by intense shouting coming from inside the house. Hasan gives us an urgent look and tells us to head for the ship. He draws his weapon and rushes into the house.

Mother and I grab the satchels and scurry down the street. We have two miles to go before reaching the harbor.

Note: Armenia today consists of approximately 11,500 sq. mi. (about the size of Maryland). Ancient Armenia consisted of approximately 60,000 sq. mi. (about the size of Illinois). The major city of Yerevan had about a population of 1.06 million in 2011. (Wikipedia: Armenia Boundaries)

Chapter 40

We make our way in a frenzied rush through the busy streets of Constantinople, stopping only now and then. The satchels are heavy, and our weary arms need a rest. We are careful not to rush by people to avoid drawing too much attention. Although we are free to move about the city, the gendarmes often pay closer attention to ethnic groups other than their own. We enter the port area just as the ship's horn blares a second time.

"Move faster before they take up the boarding plank! Mother yells while shifting her satchel to the other hand without breaking stride. I cannot believe that I am struggling to keep up with her.

We reach the ship and are relieved to see there are still a few late passengers boarding. Their access is made difficult by people who are exiting the ship after visiting with passengers onboard. This congestion on the ramp may be to our advantage.

Mother hands our documents to a port authority agent. He does not share our urgency and takes his time looking over the papers. "Let's see who we have here. Hmm, Mary Nighosian," he says, as though it is a name highlighted on his manifest list.

"Yes, is there a problem?" Mother asks.

"Perhaps," the agent responds but declines to elaborate. Instead, he motions to a gendarme close by and hands over the documents. I sense the gendarme is stationed here in case we made it to the ship.

"Mary Nighosian? Nishan Nighosian?" The gendarme gives a closer look and announces, "This morning Inspector Asid ordered that you not be allowed to board the ship. I was instructed to detain you."

Mother makes a plea. "Sir, we have proper documents showing our passage has already been paid. This is completely unfair. Please let us pass!" He is unrelenting, and we are almost out of time.

My mother overlooks something throughout this disheartening discussion. I attempt to get her attention by tugging at her coat. She ignores me and continues with the man who shows no sympathy. I persist and grab her arm.

"What is it you want, Nishan?" Her voice comes with anger for the interruption.

"What about the note from Lieutenant Hasan?" She is not the only person who immediately shifts their attention to me. The gendarme takes a keen interest in the mention of his superior officer. Mother reaches into her coat pocket and hands the note to the man.

His demeanor changes within seconds, and he informs us, "This directive cancels Inspector Asid's orders. You are free to board the ship." Just then, an ear-piercing blare rings out and we know within minutes the ship will leave Constantinople.

We hurry up the boarding plank, dragging our satchels until we step onto a lower deck. A member of the crew stops us to inquire if we need assistance in finding our room. I shake my head and tell him, "Sir, please direct us to the ship's captain."

"He's the man on the top deck," the crewman responds and points to a man in uniform. "Better hurry! We'll be leaving the port in a few minutes and the captain will be busy taking us out to sea."

We lug the satchels up several stairwells. Confused passengers seeking their rooms hinder our movement. Many are persons who booked accommodations on upper decks. We may never see them again on the voyage because they have more pleasant accommodations. Our lodging is on a lower deck with the rest of the immigrants. I take the lead trudging up each flight and repeatedly calling out, "Excuse me..." "Pardon us..." "Sorry..." Finally, we reach the top deck and approach the ship's captain.

"Sir, I am Mary Nighosian. This is my son, Nishan."

"Yes, I have been expecting you," the captain answers. "Another five minutes and I would not have been able to hold the ship in port. Welcome aboard!" The cheery greeting comes with a polite tip of his hat.

We are exhausted from the rush to the upper deck, but my mother manages to express appreciation from both of us. "Thank you; it has been a long journey." I believe she is referring to the harried rush from the house, but the captain is better informed than I expected.

"I imagine so. You are many hundreds of miles from Amasia, and I understand you did not come on a direct route." He sees the perplexed look on my face. "My friend, Dr. Demirr, told me the story about the death march. The two of you are to be admired; only a small number survive." He places a gentle hand on my shoulder.

"Yes, sir, it has been a very long journey." My response is intended to acknowledge the sacrifice of many others.

For the first time since evacuating Amasia, I feel a sense of freshness flowing through my body. The ever-present fear of being held in a concentration camp or put to death only because of my nationality has left me. I am at peace knowing that a brighter future now rests in my hands.

"The two of you are welcome to remain on the top deck with me while the ship leaves the port," the captain tells us. We eagerly accept the man's kind invitation and take a final look at the landscape of Constantinople.

Suddenly, the serenity of the moment is interrupted when a vehicle screeches to a stop on the dock. A gendarme exits and calls out as he runs toward the ship. "Hold the ramp! Hold the ramp!" The ship's captain signals the men below to allow the officer to board. He dashes up the ramp and makes his way to the top deck. I worry that all the heartache in reaching the ship has been for nothing.

"An urgent message for you, sir," the gendarme says, handing over a sealed envelope to the captain. We nervously wait as he opens the envelope and reads the enclosed letter. Our patience is tested when he does a second reading to make sure he correctly interprets the information. Meanwhile, the gendarme adds to the anxiety by keeping his eyes focused on me.

"Are you afraid, Mother?" I whisper. I know she hears even though her eyes remain fixed on the captain. He may be holding our fate in his hands.

"Shush, Nishan, this is no time to talk." Her voice softens when she tells me, "Our faith has brought us this far, and it will carry us the rest of the way."

"Thank you, officer. I believe your business here is finished," the captain tells the gendarme. "Please inform our friends that I completely understand the message." We are relieved but bewildered. The letter is mysterious to us, but not for long. The captain is about to share the information.

"There is something contained in this message from Dr. Demirr which pertains to both of you," he tells us in a serious tone. "Asid is dead."

Mother clutches my hand for support as the shocking news comes forth. She takes a moment to regain her composure, and then she asks a question for the two of us. "Are you sure?"

"Yes, it is official. There is no question about it." Our captain holds up the letter as verification. "Your enemy is no longer among the living."

I cannot accurately describe the feeling that comes over me. Perhaps it is a mixture of emotions. Relief, elation, and satisfaction seem to clash with anger and a small measure of sadness. My faith tells me not to be joyful over this death, and yet, I shed no tears. There is much more that I must learn about life. Mother takes me into her arms. The one thing that I am convinced of is her love for me.

"Strange, isn't it?" The captain captures our attention.

"What is strange, sir?" I ask, responding to the awkward question.

"Well, I find it strange that a man like Asid, a soldier who survived so many battles, would kill himself."

We are speechless as the captain continues to refer to the letter. "It says right here that the official report was completed by Lieutenant Hasan. Dr. Demirr signed it as a witness. Hmm, very strange."

~~~~~~~~~~~~~~~~~~~~~~~~~~~~~~

We lean against the railing of the top deck as Constantinople fades into the distance. The water in the bay is calm, but we know there will be rougher seas before the ship reaches America.

"Mother, our new life is about to begin."

"Yes, my son, and we will face it together." Her eyes glisten, and I hope they are tears of joy. She takes me into her arms and tells me what I must know. "You are truly a prince as is every son of Armenia. You carry on the legacy."

Mother's words inspire me as I to reflect on all the wonderful people who came before me. I will *never* forget generations of Armenians who kept an abiding faith in God, love of family, and respect for the quality of life.

What will I do in America? ... *"I will tell the story."*

...The Beginning

Epilogue

Mary and Nishan arrived at the harbor in New York after surviving the genocide of the Armenian population by the Ottoman Empire. They entered the country at Ellis Island where millions of immigrants from countries around the world began a new life.

Mary became the wife of Asadour Erganian. He adopted her son, and the boy that lived through the genocide became Nishan Erganian.

Nishan married Vartanoush Sarkisian. She was the daughter of Arixie and Dakes Sarkisian, two of the true to life characters in this novel. Nishan and 'Rose' had three daughters and a son: Mary Rose, Carolyn, Nshan and Roxy Anna.

Nishan, was a wonderful father and respected merchant during his lifetime in America. This kind and gentle man faithfully carried on the legacy of the Armenian people.

He truly was "a Prince of Armenia."

Mary and Nishan circa 1926

Nishan Erganian- successful merchant
and dedicated family man

Mary and Asadour Erganian circa 1930's

Nishan and Rose Erganian married in 1938

Arixie and Dakes Sarkisian circa 1950's

About the Author

Dr. Nshan Erganian is the author of three novels, *Prince of Armenia, Keeper of the Mountain,* and *Desperate Reunion... the Promise*; also, two short-stories, *Mom Was a Baseball Legend* and *Grandpa's Guide to Caring for Twin Grandchildren.*

A dedicated educator and administrator, he rose to leadership positions at the college level, and served as the chief executive officer for two health foundations. He was selected as Missouri's Outstanding Administrator' by the MCE Association.

He currently serves on the board of directors for the Christopher Huff Foundation. The organization is devoted to enhancing the quality of life for children with cancer and also scholarships for persons pursuing a degree in higher education. He is a member of the St. Joseph, Missouri, Writers Guild.

He and wife, Marylin, have celebrated fifty-one years of marriage. Her professional career includes service as the Administrative Assistant for a United States Congressman. She is also the co-author of *Desperate Reunion... the Promise.* The couple has two children, seven grandchildren, two great-grandchildren and counting.

Acknowledgements

The author extends his appreciation to the following persons who helped create the novel, *Prince of Armenia:*

Noray Sarkisian: Uncle Noray provided information that brought authenticity to this novel. At 95 years, his sharp mind recreated for me many of the actual events reported in the book. This 'Prince of Armenia' never ceases to remind us that every day is a gift from the Lord.

Susan (Schmidt) Smith: After several years as an outstanding teacher, Susan's talent helped to bring this story together. Her encouragement kept me on task. She is a writer's colleague and dear friend.

Samantha Fidler-Newby: Publisher, Amazing Things Press. She applied her talent as a successful writer to format of the novel. She brought the story to life in book form. A great colleague in the St. Joseph Writers Guild.

Julie Casey: Publisher, Amazing Things Press. Julie's special touch is always on display in every piece published. She keeps writers at ease maneuvers their stories through the process of turning a manuscript into a published book.

Paige (Lemon) Funk: My technology advisor. Her skills were showcased as she worked through many computer problems caused by an aging author who lacks the enthusiasm to become technology literate.

Marylin Erganian: My wife and soul mate who has collaborated with me on every novel. She is always supportive and never hesitates to let me know that I am loved. We walk through life together... and I am blessed with her presence.

Bibliography
(In order of title)

ABC of Armenian #2, Luke Arakelian (Mekhitartist Press. Cambridge, Massachusetts – 1973)

A History of the Armenian Genocide, Ronald Grigor Suny: (Princeton University Press. Princeton, New Jersey – 2015)

Ambassador Morgenthau's Story, Henry Morgenthau (Armenian General Benevolent Periodical. AGBU, April -1999)

Armenian Massacres and Turkish Tyranny, Frederick Davis Green: (Entered according to Act of Congress in 1896 by J.R. Jones, Office of the Librarian of Congress. Washington, D.C.)

100 Armenian Tales, Susie Hoogasian-Villa: (Wayne State University Press. Detroit, Michigan - 1966)

The Rebirth of Armenia, Frank Viviano: (National Geographic, March - 2004. Washington, D.C.)

Treasured Armenian Recipes, Detroit Chapter of AGBU: (Armenian General Benevolent Union, Inc. New York, N.Y. - 1966)

Yerevan, Rem Ananikyan: (Progress Publishers – Moscow)

Check out these books from
Amazing Things Press

Keeper of the Mountain by Nshan Erganian

Rare Blood Sect by Robert L. Justus

Survival In the Kitchen by Sharon Boyle

In Daddy's Hands by Julie L. Casey

MariKay's Rainbow by Marilyn Weimer

Seeking the Green Flash by Lanny Daise

Thought Control by Robert L. Justus

Bighorn by James Ozenberger

Post Exodus by Robert Christiansen

Rawnie's Mirage by Marilyn Weimer

Fall of Grace by Rachel Riley and Sharon Spiegel

Taming the Whirlwind by Lindsey Heidle

John Henry's War by Larry W. Anderson

The Brothers' Murder by Brenda Grant

A Good Life by Sarah Rowan

Desperate Reunion…the Promise by Marylin &
Nshan Erganian

Died Innocent by Don Nothstine

The Thornless Rose: Fire Blush by Samantha
Fidler-Newby

Sydney's Medallion by Marilyn Weimer

289

The Alabaster Kid/Slipknot by David Noe

The Last Destruction by L.W. Farley

Shyla's Cove by Timothy Joseph

What Dreams May Bring by Tracy Lane-Hembley

Well of Despair by Sharon Garlock Spiegel

My Own St. Nicholas by Sarah Richardson

Flint's Thunder by Marilyn Weimer

Heartland Sunset by D.K. Graham

Heartland Sunrise by D.K. Graham

Heartland Storm by D.K. Graham

Heartland: A New Kind of Storm by D.K. Graham

Fear No Evil by John J. Ensminger

Check out these Nonfiction books from

Amazing Things Press

Survival In the Kitchen by Sharon Boyle

Stop Beating the Dead Horse by Julie L. Casey

Fun Activities to Help Little Ones Talk by Kathy Blair

All American Prizefighter by Rob Calloway

Held Captive by Sharon Spiegel

Living in Someone Else's House by David Noe

Overcoming Dyslexia: One Person's Story by Jack R. Newton, Ed.S.

Survival In the Kitchen and Beyond by Sharon Boyle

Menu for a Month by Connie Condron Dow

Easy Recipes from Sandy's Heart by Sandy Smith

Teacher's Tackle Box by Dr. Joyce Piveral, Nancy Piercy, and Sue Nothstine

The Regular Joe: Refills by Jay Kerner

Parenting with Promises by Debbie Kunz

A Century of Service by Roxanne Dale

At a Loss by Steve Sewell

Made in the USA
Columbia, SC
09 February 2019